Bless This Food

Bless This Food

ancient & contemporary graces from around the world

Adrian Butash

New World Library
Novato, California

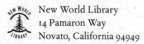 New World Library
14 Pamaron Way
Novato, California 94949

Permissions acknowledgments appear on pages 175–182.

Text design and typography by Tona Pearce Myers
Author photograph on page 189 by Annabelle Butash

Library of Congress Cataloging-in-Publication Data
    Bless this food : ancient and contemporary graces from around the world /
[compiled by] Adrian Butash. — 1st New World Library ed., completely rev.
and expanded.
        p.   cm.
Includes bibliographical references and index.
ISBN 978-1-57731-591-9 (hardcover : alk. paper)
1. Grace at meals. I. Butash, Adrian.
BL560.B55 2007
204'.33—dc22   2007025986

Originally published in 1993 by Delacorte Press. Completely revised and expanded.

First New World Library edition, October 2007

ISBN-10: 1-57731-591-X
ISBN-13: 978-1-57731-591-9

Printed in Canada on 100% postconsumer-waste recycled paper

g New World Library is a proud member of the Green Press Initiative.

10 9 8 7 6 5 4 3 2 1

To my mother and father,
who taught me how to pray

Contents

Prayers, by Origin

Acknowledgments

*B*less you all for your love and friendship: Geraldine Oberling, whose crisp mind informs every page. And blessings on my inspired agent, Amy Rennert, and estimable editorial director, Georgia Hughes. And on Letitia Anderson, Marielle Bancou-Segal, Eleonora Barna, John Barnett, Art Bass, Bob Bell, James Paul Brown, Richard Buchen, Frank Butash, Dan Clemente, Michael Coady, Barbara Fagan, Vincent Fagan, Donald Filippelli, Jan Fox, George Ledes, Rebecca MacKenzie, Sarah Phillips, Joff Pollon, Raul Roth, Gunther Ruebcke, Bill Segal, Hoyt Spelman, Norman Waterman, and Helmut Weser.

Blessings upon my family: Holly, Bob, and Anastasia; Glenn, Serra, Henry, and Charlotte; and Susannah Rake and my sweet Annabelle — no man ever had a better family.

Introduction

food blessings connect all humankind

*O*pen this book to any prayer, and you will find meaning and beauty. Food blessings provide a window to the profound spirituality that we all share and that connects us to all humankind, nature, and the infinite.

The thanks-giving food blessing is the prayer said most often in the home. This is its essential beauty. Saying a blessing before a meal can bring us closer to our brothers and sisters, parents and friends. Asking a friend to choose and recite a food blessing is a wonderful way to welcome that person into your family setting. The occasional gathering for prayer, no matter how brief, keeps the heart and mind in touch with the most fundamental of joys: belonging.

To any child who can read, this book gives the opportunity to lead the family in prayer, to participate actively in a family ritual instead of remaining a subordinate, passive member at the table. Children will also discover that food prayers provide an educational experience that stimulates the mind with many subjects: nature, history, spirituality, religion, people, and customs of other cultures throughout the world. Whether impromptu words or a formal prayer, the food blessing is a powerful medium that enriches the meaning of family and allows us to touch a higher realm of spirituality.

While prayers often derive from specific religious contexts, they may be experienced and enjoyed by all, just as religious music and fine art transcend their origins and have universal appeal. There are many nonreligious prayers that evoke spirituality by virtue of the beauty of the words and the underlying humanity that shines through.

The book of blessings I have gathered here is a spiritually nourishing basket of poetic fruit — sacred prayers from all times, for all people. Amid these words you will find the soul of humanity, the song of ages. These simple prayers of thanks are a record of humankind's unbroken relationship with God and the divine. The prayers, many of which have been uttered over eons, have never lost their power.

Sharing food is the most universal cultural experience. Expressing thanks for food was humankind's first act of worship, for food is the gift of life from above. In every culture there are sacred beliefs or divine commandments that require honoring

2

the giver of life — God or the divine principle — through acknowledging the sacred gift of food. By admitting us to his table, God became bound to us in a unique relationship. By admitting God to our table, we experience the love and beauty of that relationship.

Paleolithic rock art presents evidence of the intellectual life of our prehistoric ancestors. Humankind's earliest recorded beginnings employ food images as an expression of thankfulness to supreme beings. The Lascaux caves in southwestern France date from 30,000 years ago, and the paintings on their walls depict an array of horses, bulls, and stags — the animals of survival for the Cro-Magnons. The extraordinary art in these caves celebrates animals as both a gift from the Almighty and sustenance on earth. To me these paintings are pre-language symbolic thought, an illustration of thanks giving for life-sustaining food.

Likewise, in Egypt virtually of all of the wall paintings in ancient tombs honor the gods with gifts. Food is ever-present as both gift-offering and sustenance for the deceased pharaohs (kings) and their retinues when making the journey to the next life in the otherworld. Ancient Egyptian art contains many images of offering tables of food to the gods Osiris and Isis, depicting gifts of grapes, wine, sheaves of wheat, cakes of divine bread, duck, and fish being presented to the gods by royal priests, kings, and queens.

From humankind's earliest beginnings to today, food is the thanks-giving link and universal form of expression for gratitude to the Almighty.

Family and Guests Are a Blessing

While we recognize that religious worship has its center in churches, temples, and mosques, the family is the core of life. Gathering together to say a blessing before eating food is a wonderful way to bring God into our houses, right to the table with our families. Worship should be a vital part of every family's life, but our modern, busy lifestyles often leave little time for regular religious worship. Today, the notion of the family is under siege by a barrage of social ills, and family life may be disrupted by parents' absence as they work two jobs, by divorce, or by frequent separation resulting from business travel that takes parents away from home.

The family food blessing is a perfect and reverent way for the family to experience a direct kinship with the Almighty. A grace's spiritual power can be felt as a profound sense of reality. God is present. A family praying together is a beautiful thing — a wonderful blessing all its own. When we say a grace at the table before eating, we give thanks for our togetherness, our blessings, and our happiness. For loved ones who are deceased, for friends and family who are far away, a grace said at the table that mentions their names is a magical way to honor them and have them rejoin the table in a sublime sense. Moreover, we should all say a grace and include a thankful mention of our servicemen and servicewomen. They will hear you.

Children need prayer models to see, hear, and experience in order to learn from the ritual. The table blessing is among the easiest and most enjoyable for children to partake in — coming as it does just before the family feast. *Bless This Food* has several blessings that young people will enjoy reciting for the family, one-minute performances that all will remember and cherish.

There are four principal types of thanks-giving graces: the silent grace, the spoken grace, the sung grace, and the signed grace. I thought it would be nice to include an adult's and a child's signed grace (see "A Grace in American Sign Language" on page 172 and "A Child's Grace in American Sign Language" on page 173). They have a beauty all their own. See for yourself.

This book may be an especially useful tool when a guest or visitor at the table is called on to say grace, since many people are not comfortable with impromptu speaking. Keep the book near the table to provide guests with a ready script. They will find it easy to choose a blessing and then honor the occasion with a reading. A food blessing transforms everyone into a circle of friends.

Origins of Gratitude for Food

Consider: The first interhuman act of the newborn child is to experience satisfaction through food. In the first hour of life, our senses may transmit ephemeral sight, sound, or touch quanta, but it is the initial ingestion of milk from the mother that constitutes the first interhuman act: life-sustaining nourishment. The immediate response to this nourishment is a systemic and psychic satisfaction, and the hunger-gratification cycle begins at this instant and continues throughout life. The just-born infant's first human experience is a "gift" of milk in response to its sucking instinct and need for food, a gratifying experience that affects the infant's psyche on its deepest level. This *gratia* (thanks) experience is imprinted on the newborn's uninscribed mind and is the primordial unconscious analogue to voiced prayer. Our first common human emotional experience is the *gratia* response for food.

The ritualized saying of food prayers in thanks for God's bounty is an experience of acculturation in social and religious practices. This imposition of formal prayer-saying is a confirmation of our first primal food experience. It gives form to expressing thankfulness that reaches back to our first minutes of life and is something inherently cognate within us. The *gratia* experience we encounter as infants is transformed and intellectualized over time into an appreciation of food as both spiritual and physical nourishment that we acknowledge in the *gratia* prayer.

The sacred texts of the world, such as the Christian and Hebrew Bibles, the Koran, the Lotus Sutra, and the Hindu Vedic corpus, have a profound quality in common. What marks them as sacred is their treatment as holy documents possessing supreme authority and power by virtue of their divine origin. Sacred texts are those created directly by God or revealed to humankind or recorded by holy prophets.

Through the centuries, rebbes, monks, and saints have orally passed down such sacred texts as the Pali canon, the sacred scripture of Theravada Buddhism, and the Torah. The latter originally was forbidden to be written down and was memorized by tannas, the flawless "repeaters" of the text. Sacred texts are immutable and are considered to be closed texts, which cannot be altered or revised.

A distinguishing feature of a sacred text is its beneficence to humanity. While not all food prayers are sacred (and some in this anthology are not), they all possess some kind of beneficial power for humankind.

For individuals whose intellectual interest is in what Paul Verlaine has called "mere literature," the compelling beauty of these thanks-giving food prayers reveals the noble spirituality of humanity. Prayer is how human beings relate to God, nature, and their place in the divine order of things.

Prayer is the principal channel we use in our search for ultimate meaning. Thanks-giving food prayers embody religious and social contexts, encompassing myth, sacred doctrine, rituals, and social and cultural practices.

Scriptural Sources and Texts

The gods command prayers of thanks for food. The Bible has several citations that illustrate this command, for example: "And thou shall eat and be satisfied, and bless the Lord your God" (Deut. 8:10). The divine origin of the words of the Koran is better appreciated if you understand that the Koran is to Muslims what Jesus — not the Bible — is to Christianity. A verse from the Koran, the words of Allah, the God of Islam, as recorded under divine guidance by the Prophet Muhammad instructs Muslims on the sacred origins of food and the requirement for food prayers: "Eat of your Lord's provision, and give thanks to Him" (34:15).

The theological notion of grace infuses the meaning of

thankfulness. Grace is the unmerited love of God and the presence of God in us. This presence of divine love is gratuitous. The word *gratuitous* (given freely) comes from the Latin *gratuitus* (grateful) and derives from the Latin word for thanks (*gratia*), which is found in many languages, such as Old French, *gratus* (thankful), and Sanskrit, *grnati* (sing praise). *Grace* in Greek is *charis* (charisma). *Charismata* is the power of the Holy Spirit. A grace is the thanks-to-God utterance before or after a meal. Food has always been recognized as the unmerited gift from God. Grace is the divine reality underlying all religion and faith — that is, God's loving generosity. In the Hebrew scriptures it is *hesed* (loving kindness). In the Tao it is found in the love of the Hindu triad Brahma, Vishnu, and Shiva. In Christian theology, grace is the human-transcendent activity of God in every creature.

Whether that expression of thanks (*gratia*) for the gift of spiritual and physical food is voiced in a tribal ritualized saying or uttered silently or sung eloquently, a person's intrinsic spiritual nature imposes the recognition that the very food before him or her is sacred and mysterious and comes to him or her from the beyond.

While this book is a collection of blessings that civilization has preserved, there are other momentous prayers of thanks that are documented but whose actual words are not known. Two intriguing examples are two prayers of thanks that, according to the Bible, Jesus offered at the Last Supper. We don't know if the prayers were voiced or silent. Jesus' exact words (if they were spoken) were not recorded by the authors of the New Testament.

In the course of the Last Supper, the Bible tells us, "Jesus gave thanks" to God in heaven. The first grace was intoned before Jesus drank the wine, and the second divine *gratia* given before he ate the bread. These two thanks-giving prayers of Jesus are sacred mysteries.

Gratia in Jewish Sources

The Hebrew word for prayer is *tefilah*. The most important aspect of any Jewish prayer is the introspection it offers — a moment when we look inside ourselves and evaluate our relationship to God. The Yiddish word for "praying" is *daven*, a word whose origins in Latin and English mean "divine." Deuteronomy 8:10 commands that when a Jew eats he must bless the Lord with this prayer.

The three main Israelite feasts recorded in the Bible were, in part, harvest festivals, for which multitudes of Jews brought fruits and vegetables to the temple in Jerusalem. These feasts were Pesach, at the beginning of the barley harvest; Shavout, in summer at the end of the wheat harvest; and Sukkot, in autumn during the gathering of grapes and other cultivated fruits. The Mishnah, too, shows the reverence for food and food blessings. Of the six major sections of the Mishnah — the first collection of Jewish law (AD 200) and one of the earliest surviving works of rabbinic literature — one section is devoted to seeds and agriculture, another to festivals. Food is rampant in Jewish text and festivals. Elal (Hebrew *elul*, "to reap" or "harvest"), for example, is the twelfth month in the Jewish year.

In the Old Testament the breaking of bread together symbolized the immutable bonds among all people. The Covenant with God was reaffirmed through deeply profound meals and feasts. Even the Hebrew word for "covenant" (*b'rith*) has etymological origins in the Hebrew word meaning "to eat." The Birkat Hazan, the grace said before a meal, is recited before eating the first morsel of bread. It is an ancient Jewish prayer (55) that has been intoned in Jewish homes over centuries.

The Jewish liturgy is full of the idea of divine grace interceding to aid humanity. *Grace* in Hebrew is "Ahabah Rabbah," and *thanks giving* is "Shemoneh Esreh." The liturgy requires separate blessings (*b'rachot*) for various categories of food. The blessing over bread (the *hamotzi*) differs from that over cakes and cooked grains; fruits and vegetables have their own blessings, as do wine and fragrances. Inviting poor people to have food with you makes your table an altar and the meal itself into an atonement. Martin Buber helps us realize that our very table is sacred: "One eats in holiness and the table becomes an altar."

The Dead Sea Scrolls document another fascinating prayer of thanks that was a sacred rite of the Essenes, the authors of the scrolls. (*Essene* means "pious one.") This ancient esoteric Jewish sect existed from the second century BC to the first century AD and, as a result, the scrolls have been unaffected by either Christian or rabbinical censorship (rabbinic teachers did not permit religious writings to enter Jewish posterity if they did not conform to strict orthodoxy). The scrolls provide an insight into ancient, pre–Christian-Jewish literature, customs, and beliefs. Prayer 8 is a wonderful blessing I composed that is based on fragments of the Dead Sea Scrolls known as the Thanksgiving hymns.

One of the key concepts of Jewish eschatology (final days) is the Day of Judgment. A chapter in the scrolls known as "The Messianic Rule" gives a visionary description of the end of the world and the coming of the Messiah. It details the prescribed conduct for members of the community in celebrating this miraculous event. At the end of the world there will be a great feast. The Messiah will sit at the head of the table, and before him will sit the chiefs of the clans of Israel, the wise men, and all others. The congregation will eat and drink new wine, but not before a prayer of thanks. A priest will bless the firstfruits of bread and wine on the Day of Atonement, and then the Messiah will hold his hand over the bread, and each man and woman will be required to recite his or her own blessing. In this remarkably beautiful last rite, the final act of human beings will be to create their own blessings, to be uttered before the Messiah.

Gratia in Sumerian Sources

Historians acknowledge the Sumerian civilization as the very first (3000 BC). The Sumerians lived in Mesopotamia, later known as Babylonia, the cradle of agricultural development. The Sumerian and Middle Eastern pantheon had many gods of food, crops, and abundance, whose thanks-giving prayers did not survive the ages. This list included the gods Abu, Baal, Dagon, Mot, Nikkal, Ninib, Ninsar, and Tammuz. Sumerian mythology and culture were the source of the Babylonian,

Assyrian, Phoenician, and biblical customs and rituals that evolved into Judaism, Christianity, and Islam.

As you'll see in prayer 4, a Sumerian artifact discovered in the mid-twentieth century revealed that giving thanks for food was a practice integral to the culture.

Gratia in Muslim Sources

For Muslims, confessing the proper beliefs is the foundation on which life is built. Islam is wholly monotheistic. The *shahadah*, which means "to bear witness," is the Islamic creed recited by every Muslim and is the Muslim declaration of belief in the one-ness of God and in Muhammad as his final prophet. God com-municates to Muslims through the Koran, which is Muhammad's recitations, inspired by God and written down by his followers. The Koran is considered to be the flawless revelations of God. Muslims believe angels are messengers of God and that the angel Gabriel delivered the words of the Koran to Muhammad. Muhammad died without naming a successor, and the dis-agreement over the principles of naming a successor led to the formation of two major sects: Shia — those who accepted Ali as successor — and Sunni, the traditional majority, who ac-cepted Mu'awiyah as the next leader.

Muslims' thanks-giving prayer is the *basmalah*, bismi-Llahi-r Rahmani-r-Rahim ("In the name of God, the Merciful, the Compassionate"). Reciting the *basmalah* is the equivalent of say-ing grace, and it is never omitted before a Muslim meal. And a meal is never ended without uttering the *hamdalah* (also known colloquially as the *hamdullah*), meaning "praise God," the required ending response to the *basmalah*. The Prophet is clear on the motivation for saying grace: "If you are thankful, surely I will increase you" (Koran 14:7).

Gratia in Hindu Sources

A Hindu is an adherent of the philosophies and scriptures of Hinduism, the religious, philosophical, and cultural system that originated on the Indian subcontinent. Hindus believe in the Vedas, the most important of which are the Mahabharata and the Ramayana, written in the ancient language of Sanskrit. These scriptural texts of Hinduism originated in ancient India. As the world's oldest religion, one that inspired others, Hinduism is "the mother of all religions." The Vedas are the oldest surviving texts in the world.

While not a food blessing, the Yajurved — one of the four Hindu Vedas composed in the early Iron Age, around the tenth century BC — acknowledges the sun as our primal source of nourishment. This blessing is a dazzling and beautiful voice from humankind's earliest history: "O nourishing Sun, solitary traveler, controller, source of life for all creatures, spread your light and subdue your dazzling splendor so that I may see your blessed Self. Even that very Self am I!"

Fasting is common among most Hindus. They fast on certain days of the week in accordance with their beliefs, to appease certain deities. Most fasting Hindus abstain from eating meat and live on only fruits and milk. Fasting is seen as a form of penance (*tapasya*), a means to develop a close bond with the Supreme Being.

Hindu prayer cleanses the food of three impurities, those caused by contaminants in the vessel, in the food stuffs, and in the process of cooking. It is necessary to purify the food in this way, for pure food goes into the making of a pure mind.

In the Hindu belief, food cannot be eaten unless it is first offered to God. It then becomes *prasad* (sanctified or observed as holy), that is, food blessed by God. Hinduism puts great emphasis on the loving reliance upon God. An example of this is seen in prayer 7 from the Bhagavad Gita (Song of the Lord), Hinduism's most sacred religious text. The Gita is found in the Mahabharata, an extraordinary Sanskrit epic that dates from the second century BC. Another sublime prayer from antiquity is a paean to Annapurna, a beneficent goddess who, as mother, nourishes all things (prayer 12).

Gratia in Christian Sources

The Old Testament and New Testament of the Bible abound with examples of blessings and incorporate into their liturgy food-related rituals, ceremonies, and metaphors. The New Testament, for example, records the sharing of food on numerous occasions. In Luke's Gospel there are thirty-one such citations. There are fourteen in John, twenty-six in Mark, and twenty in Matthew. Throughout Corinthians, food and its consumption occupy an important theological position and are mentioned by Paul twenty-two times.

The Last Supper, the final meal eaten by Jesus with his apostles before the Crucifixion, traditionally has been called the Passover meal. For Christians, the Lord's Prayer (prayer 41), recited at the Lord's Supper, is a universal thanks-giving prayer, with its imagery of gratefulness for life-sustaining daily bread. Theologically, the Eucharist is the Christian sacrament commemorating the Last Supper.

The word *Eucharist* is derived from the Greek *eucharistia* (thanks giving). In the celebration of Holy Communion, the consecrated bread and wine are transformed into the body and blood of Jesus Christ. "He that eateth my flesh, and drinketh my blood, dwelleth in me, and I in him" (John 6:56).

Gratia in Chinese Sources

China's religious beliefs are principally based on the worship of certain deities and on ancestor worship. Fundamental to Chinese dogma is that heaven is Yang and earth is Yin — and both exist in harmonious balance. In Chinese thought, there must be harmony in Yin (female) and Yang (male) principles if there is to be peace in the family. Chinese children grow up in homes that honor the father and mother. This balance and harmony are present in the Tao (Dao) — the Way of the universe.

Food and associated prayers play a central role in religions of the Far East. Confucius, a contemporary of Buddha and the most widely known sage, founded Confucianism in the sixth century BC, one of the two major Chinese ideologies. The other is Taoism (from *Tao* meaning "the Way"). Taoism is based on the annual rotation of the seasons and the harmony and balance of nature.

Whereas the religions of India emphasize karma and reincarnation, the religions of China emphasize reverence for one's ancestors — the family. At the Tasze, the great sacrifice site in China's huge Altar Park (location of the largest altar in the world), offerings of food, rice spirits, and other gifts are placed on the altar, and the spirit of heaven is invited by means of a sacred hymn to descend to the altar and honor one's ancestors and the gods. Sie and Tsih, for example, the gods of millet and corn, are worshipped in spring and autumn sacrifices. The modern, expedient Chinese *gratia* before the banquet meal, *Duo xie, duo xie* (A thousand thanks, a thousand thanks), is a result of the cultural evolution of worship chanted to the many food gods of Chinese antiquity, among them Chi Ming, Ching Ling Tzu, and Chung Tso. A witty and sophisticated saying in Chinese cultural circles today that has the elegance of poetry is an observation made by the contemporary philosopher Ren Yi Shi Wei Tian: 人以食为天 , or "People perceive food to be almost like God."

Certain Chinese dining customs are worth mentioning here. Dinner invitations are sent in a red envelope, red being the color of festivity. Seating at the table should be spontaneous, so that no party is left standing while another is seated. After the meal, departing guests should be escorted all the way to the door: "If you escort a man at all, escort him all the way."

There is a wonderful Chinese poem, "Inviting Guests"

(prayer 57), dating from circa AD 273, that is as modern and meaningful for today as when it was written over seventeen hundred years ago. It is a wonderful glimpse of ancient Chinese hospitality, which we can see is identical to our own sense of sharing food and drink, and experiencing the sublime pleasures of friendship.

The most conspicuous element of European poetry is its preoccupation with love. The Chinese poet deals not with love, but friendship. Chinese poetry is influenced by the "Three Teachings," based on Confucianism, Taoism, and Buddhism, which taught about the importance of being loyal, unselfish, and courteous. Filial piety is considered the first virtue in Chinese culture; a respect and love for one's parents and ancestors.

Gratia in Japanese Sources

Shinto is the old native religion of Japan that reveres ancestors and nature spirits. Derived from the Chinese Shen-Tao (way of the gods), Shinto's central belief is that Kami, God, is the sacred power that infuses animate and inanimate things.

Amaterasu, the beneficent sun goddess, is the most eminent of the Shinto deities. The sun has been an object of veneration in many religions, such as that of the Egyptians. Amaterasu taught humankind the cultivation of food. Inari is the grain god. Shinto's adherents believe in the power of spoken prayer, and among these are *norito* prayers, those that petition the gods for good harvests.

The Setsubun ceremony celebrates the start of a new

season of seeds and planting. Its rites involve Neolithic rituals that survive today in techno-futurist Japan. A cornucopia of sacred treasures — rice, cakes, fish, and vegetables — is placed on the altar to express thanks for the bounty of the earth.

The Japanese religions, like those of the Chinese, honor millions of ancestors. Many families have a *butsudan*, a center for observing reverence for ancestors and departed members of the family.

The early Stone Age peoples who inhabited what we know as the Japanese islands appeared there as early as 30,000 BC, according to fossil DNA samples. In the Stone Age, the Jomon and Yayoi peoples developed a distinct culture and worshipped *kami no michi*, "the way of the gods." Buddhism came to Japan from Korea in the sixth century. Japanese today can participate simultaneously in Shintoism and Buddhism without conflict.

Buddhism focuses on the teachings of Gautama Buddha, who was born Siddhārtha Gautama in the fifth century BC. According to Buddha, any person can become enlightened through the study of his words, or dharma, and by putting them into practice — by leading a virtuous, moral life and purifying the mind. Unlike many religions, Buddhism has no single central text, one that is universally referred to by all Buddhist traditions.

Buddhism's history is rich with reverence for food and thankfulness for its nourishment. The great prince Gautama Sakyamuni experienced full enlightenment while sipping a cup of rice milk as he meditated on the doctrine of nirvana under the tree of enlightenment, the bodhi tree. Buddhists have offered prayers of blessing for everything from the cultivation of crops to the dedication of each plate of food for the betterment of humanity. As exemplified by the Buddhist prayers in this book, food can be truly blessed only when the person giving thanks has lived a life of service to both the universe that has provided the food and to those who suffer and are without food. Buddhism expresses thankfulness for food by its adherents' "vow to live a life which is worthy to receive it" (prayer 129). A wonderful Buddhist mealtime prayer is: "The food is the gift of the whole universe. Each morsel is a sacrifice of life. May I be worthy to receive it. May the energy in this food give me the strength to transform my unwholesome qualities into wholesome ones. I am grateful for this food. May I realize the Path of Awakening, for the sake of all beings."

Gratia in Native American Sources

Native American Indian tribes share a common reverence for the earth and all its bounty. Animals, harvests, and water must be accepted with thankfulness in rituals and prayers. Respect for the food gift is often expressed by asking a plant or animal that must be used for food for forgiveness for taking its life and by explaining why its death was necessary (prayer 127). In Native American thought, human beings are the earth's dependents, not its masters.

Food as Offerings to God

The development of civilization is synonymous in every sense with the growth of agriculture. The cultivation of crops predates the invention of the wheel and writing. Belief in the power of the firstfruits and grains of the season has provided the world with many rituals, beliefs, and festivals. The festival calendars of antiquity were based on agriculture, and our modern calendars descended from these agricultural calendars.

The cultivation of plants for food, as opposed to the use of wild plants growing naturally in the environment, marked human beings' evolution from food users to producers of food.

All civilizations and all religions throughout all ages have associated food with God or gods; all primitive nonbelievers have associated food with a supernatural power or spirits. All recognize the earth's bounty — crops and other forms of food — as a reflection of divine goodness.

Food prayers to the gods have many purposes. They make one's wishes known, honor the dead in order to show reverence for life, and reconcile God or the gods with humanity in order to bring good fortune to human beings or to assure their place in the afterlife. The recognition of the earth as sacred manifests itself in the ritual and religious life of communities, by means of petitional prayers said by the laborers, by chants at seed planting and crop proliferation, by ceremonies for laying out plots, by transmittal of family tradition, and by reflection on the concept of home and hearth. Central to all cultures and religions, food is a sacred gift that forms the supreme and universal bond of all friendship.

The world's quest for happiness operates within a context of reverence for God through a sacred link to food. In this uncertain age when ethnic differences divide people, we should strive to embrace our common humanity, which is expressed so succinctly in food prayers. These prayers talk to us with the wisdom of the ages and teach us that we are all one family, all one mystical soul. Food prayers throughout history may be seen as evidence of our profound sense of awe in the face of the infinite.

There are many ways to analyze and classify food prayers: by country, by culture, by language, by religion, by God, by food, by sacred imagery — to name a few. A definitive analysis of food prayers is beyond the scope of this book, however. I have chosen to include here both prayers and some texts that are not necessarily prayers but that nevertheless have great spiritual quality, literary merit, and eloquence in expressing humankind's profound debt to God. In some cases, the prayers in this book are excerpts of larger pieces, though I have not explicitly identified them as such in the text.

I have arranged the prayers, with a few exceptions, chronologically, from antiquity to contemporary times. In the cases of the exceptions, I decided that certain prayers had a flow and mood in their beauty and meaning and seemed to fit better thematically where I placed them. This decision was mine alone.

When your family and friends gather at the table, you will find starting your meal with a blessing will enhance the experience for all who are gathered. The book provides an easy way for anyone, young or old, to create a special, spiritual moment that everyone present will enjoy and remember. A circle of friends is the ultimate blessing.

Prayers

Prayer 1

Let me meditate on the glorious Supreme Being, the Sun,
which brightens all the three worlds —
the Heaven, the Earth, and the Nether land.
May He enlighten our hearts and direct our
      understanding.

— The Gayatri Hymn (circa 1500 BC)

The Gayatri Hymn, the holiest verse in the Rig-Veda (III. 4.10), ad-
dresses the sun, the Supreme Being, who was usually personified as a
goddess, the wife of Brahma and the metaphorical mother of all. The
sun is a metaphor for divinity, being the generative support for life on
earth and the provider of food.

Said to have been inscribed on dry leaves, the Vedas — the sacred
scriptures of Hinduism — are the most ancient ritual utterances of the
early Aryans of India. The name of this particular hymn comes from the
Sanskrit gai, *meaning to sing. The hymn is also known as the Gayatri*
Mantra. The word mantra *means incantation. A mantra can be a one-*
syllable word or a few words, a sentence or a few sentences.

Here with flowers I interweave my friends.
Let us rejoice!
Our common house is the earth.
I am come too, here I am standing;
now I am going to forge songs,
make a stem flowering with songs,
oh my friend!
God has sent me as a messenger.
I am transformed into a poem.

— Nahuatl blessing (circa 1300 BC)

The Nahuatl Indians of Mexico considered food sacred, a gift from the Sky Father and Earth Mother. Quetzalcoatl was a feathered serpent deity who represented earth and vegetation, and was important in art and religion throughout Mesoamerica for over two thousand years, a period encompassing the preclassical era, before the Spanish conquest. Civilizations worshipping the feathered serpent included the Olmec, Mixtec, Toltec, and Aztec, all of whom adopted it from the Mayan people.

Prayer 3

I am food, I am food, I am food.

I am the food-eater, I am the food-eater, I am the food-eater.

I am the combining agent, I am the combining agent, I am the combining agent.

I am the first-born of the world-order, earlier than the gods, in the center of immortality.

Whoso gives me, he surely does save thus.

I, who am food, eat the eater of food. I have overcome the world. I am brilliant like the sun.

— Mystical chant from the Upanishads (circa 900 BC)

The Upanishads are part of the Vedas, the sacred scriptures of Hinduism. Composed over several centuries, the Upanishads illuminate the doctrine of Brahman — the ultimate reality of pure consciousness — and the identity of Brahman with atman, the inner self of man. These scriptures were transmitted orally in Sanskrit through the ages and were considered poetic liturgy. The Upanishads also contain the most definitive explications of aum (OM), the divine oral word, the cosmic vibration that underlies all existence.

Prayer 4

On the day the seed breaks through the ground...
say a prayer to Ninkilim.

— Nunurta (circa 1700 BC)

In an ancient Sumerian site called Nippur, a small inscribed tablet that dates from 1700 BC was unearthed in 1949. It is known in anthropological circles as the first farmers' almanac because it records agricultural advice offered by a father to his son. Along with practical instructions, the father has recorded the requirement that one must say a thanks-giving-for-food prayer, a commandment laid down by Nunurta, son of the "true farmer" Enlil, a principal Sumerian deity.

Prayer 5

Author of my well-being,
source of knowledge,
fount of holiness, height of glory,
all-mightiness of eternal splendor!
    I shall choose that which
He shall have taught me
and I shall rejoice in that which
He shall have appointed unto me.
    When I put forth my hands and my feet,
I shall bless His Name;
when I go out or when I go in,
when I sit down or when I rise up,
and upon my bed shall I sing unto Him.
I shall bless Him with the offering
which comes forth from my lips
for the sake of all which He has established
unto men, and before I lift up my hands to partake
of the delicious fruits of the earth.

— Dead Sea Scrolls (second century BC–first century AD)

*The Dead Sea Scrolls, a collection of biblical Hebrew documents,
were recorded on parchment by a Jewish sect known as the Essenes of
Qumran and later hidden in jars in caves. The scrolls occupy a place
in the history of biblical writing and poetry and are important to scholars of both the Old Testament and the New Testament.*

The Essenes were a pious sect who dressed in white and ate com-
munal meals at which a priest said grace before eating. It was unlaw-
ful for anyone to taste the food before grace was said. Both Josephus,
a first-century Jewish historian, and Philo, a Hellenized Jewish philoso-
pher, recorded accounts of the Essenes' communal meetings, meals, and
religious celebrations. The tribes were most probably strict vegetarians
who ate mainly bread, wild roots, and fruits.

Prayer 6

Offerings are made to thee,
Oxen are slain to thee,
Great festivals are kept for thee,
Pure flames are offered to thee.

— Egyptian prayer (3100 BC–AD 400)

Ancient Egyptians prayed to Hapi, the Nile god of nourishment,
petitioning for the flood that would enrich the fields. Each and every
year, Hapi would increase the Nile so that it flooded, depositing rich
soil on the farmlands, allowing the Egyptians to grow crops — and sur-
vive. His name means "Running One," referring to the current of the
Nile. Occasionally, the annual flood was said to be the arrival of Hapi.
In hieroglyphics he is was often pictured carrying offerings of food or
pouring water.

O Lord of the universe
Please accept all this food
It was given by you
Let it be of service to all
Only you can bless it

— Bhagavad Gita (500 BC)

The Bhagavad Gita is the "Song of the Lord," also known as the "Song of the Divine One." Written in Sanskrit, the poem comes from the Mahabharata, one of the greatest religious classics of Hinduism. The Gita is often described as a concise guide to Hindu philosophy. One Hindu concept teaches that food should not be eaten unless it is first offered to God. It then becomes prasad — *blessed by God. The Bhagavad Gita is one of the most compelling and important texts of the Hindu tradition. It is considered by scholars to be one of the world's greatest religious and spiritual scriptures.*

I thank Thee, O Lord,
>because Thou hast bound me in the bundle of life.

I thank Thee, O Lord,
>because Thou has saved me from the pit.

I thank Thee, O Lord,
>because Thou has gladdened me with thy
>Covenant.

I thank Thee, O Lord,
>because Thou hast set thine eye on me.

— The Thanksgiving Hymns, from the Dead Sea Scrolls
(second century BC–first century AD)

I composed this original thanks-giving blessing from the exact texts of couplets taken from a group of sixty-six fragments of eight devotional poems in biblical Hebrew. The eight devotional poems are characterized by the identical formulaic opening line of each one, "I thank Thee, O Lord." These eight poems are recorded in the Scroll of the Hodayat (thanks giving).

The Dead Sea Scrolls are of great religious and historical significance, as they are among the very few known surviving biblical documents written before AD 100. The parchment scrolls, discovered in a cave in Qumran in 1947 by a shepherd boy, were wrapped in linen and stored in jars. They include texts from the Hebrew Bible, a term that refers to the common portions of the Jewish and Christian biblical canons.

The spiritually minded,
who eat in the spirit of service,
are freed from all their sins;
but the selfish,
who prepare food for their own satisfaction,
eat sin.

Living creatures are nourished by food,
and food is nourished by rain;
rain itself is the water of life,
which comes from selfless worship and service.

— Bhagavad Gita (500 BC)

The Gita illuminates Krishna's teachings, especially the grace of God. Sri Krishna (Sri is a holy title similar to "Lord") has been called the Christ of India owing to the remarkable parallels between the lives of Krishna and Jesus. As implied by this hymn from the Gita, any sacrifice performed without regard for scriptural instructions, without distribution of prasadam *(spiritual food), without chanting of Vedic hymns, without remunerations to the priests, and without faith is considered to be the result of ignorance. Hence, it is essential to offer food to God in the form of prayer, so that impurities do not afflict one's mind.*

We thank you, Father,
for the life and knowledge you have revealed to us
through your child Jesus.
Glory be yours through all ages.
As grain once scattered on the hillside
was in this broken bread made one,
so from all lands may we be gathered
into your kingdom by your Son.

— The Didache (circa AD 70–150)

The name Didache *comes from* didactic, *a Greek word related to "doctrine." It refers to the "Teaching of the Two Ways," exemplified in this passage: "There are two ways, one of life and one of death, and there is a great difference between the two ways" (chap. 1:1). The Didache is the oldest Christian literature outside of the New Testament. A church manual of early Christian practice — that is, a catechism — it included advice on aspects of church life, including piety, prayers, and food matters. Catechisms are doctrinal manuals in the form of questions followed by answers, a format that enhanced learning and memorization. The "early Christian" period extends from the time of Jesus' death, in approximately AD 33, to 325, when the First Council of Nicea was formed. Christianity grew out of a sect composed of the followers of Jesus during the period of the second temple, built in the first century.*

Ishvari, who ever giveth food,
Bestower of happiness to all,
Who advanceth all people,
Presiding Devi over the city of Kashi,
Vessel of mercy, grant me aid.

— From the Mahabharata (200 BC–AD 200)

The Mahabharata, the Sanskrit epic of India, whose title means "Great India," is the longest single poem in the world, containing seventy-four thousand verses, plus long prose passages of 1.8 million words total. It is the foremost source of information on classical Indian civilization and Hindu ideals. The scope and grandeur of the Mahabharata is best summarized by a quotation from the beginning of its first parva *(section): "What is found here, may be found elsewhere. What is not found here, will not be found elsewhere."* Devi *is the Sanskrit word for Goddess. She is synonymous with Shakti, the female aspect of divinity, and is the provider of spiritual and physical nourishment.*

Prayer 12

O Devi, clad in fine garment.
Ever giver of rice, Sinless One,
Who delights in the dance of Shiva.
O Annapurna! Obeisance to thee.

— Hymns to the Goddess (circa 200 BC)

This hymn comes from the Tantrasara, an ancient Vedic Sanskrit text. In the Hindu faith, the goddess Devi is creator and nourisher of the world, a role analogous to that of the Christian "Mother of God." She bears the fruit of all knowledge. The goddess Annapurna is the Hindu goddess of food and cooking. Rice here means all life-sustaining food in general. In sculpture and drawings, Annapurna is represented as the goddess who holds in one hand a jeweled vessel containing food and, in the other, a spoon to distribute the food among her devotees. She has the power to give food to an unlimited number of people. The name Annapurna *literally means "one who is full of food." In India, images of Annapurna are often displayed anywhere people eat.*

If beings knew, as I know, the result of giving and
 sharing,
they would not eat without having given,
nor would they allow the stain of meanness
to obsess them and take root in their minds.
Even if it were their last morsel, their last mouthful,
they would not enjoy eating without having shared it,
if there were someone to share it with.

— Teachings of the Buddha (fifth century BC)

*This prayer comes from the Itivuttaka. Siddhārtha Gautama (Buddha)
lived as a prince in a wealthy family in Nepal for thirty years. His en-
counters with a crippled man (representing old age), a diseased man
(illness), a decaying corpse (death), and an ascetic (a life of poverty)
motivated him to abandon his inheritance and dedicate his life to re-
lieving suffering. He attained enlightenment after a little girl gave him,
the future Buddha, some rice to eat. It was the meal that allowed him
to complete his goal of attaining nirvana as he meditated under the
bodhi tree.*

*His teachings focused on the Four Noble Truths (especially on the
idea that suffering is part of existence) and the Noble Eightfold Path
(right thought, right understanding, right speech, right action, right
livelihood, right effort, right mindfulness, and right concentration).
Theravada Buddhism strongly emphasizes the practice of giving as an
essential religious act and identifies generosity as one of the most admired spiritual goals.*

Prayer 14

May the blessing of God rest upon you,
May his peace abide with you,
May his presence illuminate your heart
Now and forevermore.

— Sufi blessing (seventh century)

Sufism, which dates from the seventh century, is the esoteric dimension of the Islamic faith, an inner spiritual path to a mystical union with God. Sufism originated in the Koran and is compatible with mainstream Islamic theology. Around AD 1000, the early Sufi literature, in the form of manuals, treatises, discourses, and poetry, became the historic record of Sufi thinking and meditations.

Sufism is based on the teachings of Muhammad and emphasizes a love for humanity. Sufi ideas infuse Arab and Persian poetry. Adherents of Islam belong to numerous sects; the Sunni and Shia are the two main branches.

O God, give me light in my heart
and light in my tongue
and light in my hearing
and light in my sight
and light in my feeling
and light in all my body
and light before me
and light behind me.

Give me, I pray Thee,
light upon my right hand
and light upon my left hand
and light above me
and light beneath me.
O Lord, increase light within me
and give me light
and illuminate me.

— Ascribed to Muhammad (circa AD 570–632)

Muhammad was an Arab religious, political, and military leader who founded the Islamic faith and united the tribes of the Arabian Peninsula into a federation of allied tribes with its capital at Medina. At age forty, he reported receiving revelations from God through the angel Gabriel. These revelations were documented by his followers and became the basis for the Koran, which is considered to be the direct word of God. Muhammad is the most important prophet of God (Allah). For scholars of Islamic law, he is the legislator-jurist who defined ritual observance; for the mystic, he is the ideal seeker of spiritual perfection; for the philosopher and statesman, he is a role model as both a conqueror and a just ruler; for ordinary Muslims, he is a model of God's grace and salvation.

Prayer 16

Blessed are you, Lord.
You have fed us from our earliest days;
you give food to every living creature.
Fill our hearts with joy and delight.
Let us always have enough
and something to spare for works of mercy
in honor of Christ Jesus, our Lord.
Through him, may glory, honor, and power be yours
    forever.

— Fourth-century Christian prayer

Praise we the Lord
Of the heavenly kingdom,
God's power and wisdom,
The works of His hand;
As the Father of glory,
Eternal Lord,
Wrought the beginning
Of all His wonders!
Holy Creator!
Warden of men!
First, for a roof,
O'er the children of earth,
He established the heavens,
And founded the world,
And spread the dry land
For the living to dwell in.
Lord Everlasting!
Almighty God!

— Caedmon (AD 680)

This grace is "Caedmon's Hymn," named for a lay brother at an English monastery who feared the custom of singing at meals. One evening, Caedmon retired to the stable out of shame, as he had often done, and as he slept he had a vision that called him by name and bade him sing. "I cannot sing, and therefore I left the feast," he protested, to which the vision replied, "Sing to me, however, sing of Creation." At this,

Caedmon began to sing verses inspired by God's urging. In the morning Caedmon recited his story and his verses to the learned men of the monastery, and all agreed that he had received a divine gift. This grace, composed in Northumbrian dialect, holds a distinctive place in English poetry as the earliest known text in English.

Prayer 18

Zeus, beginning of all things,
Of all things the leader,
Zeus, to thee a libation I pour,
Of hymns the beginning.

— Terpander of Lesbos (circa 676 BC)

This hymn composed by Terpander of Lesbos, a Greek poet and musician, is addressed to Zeus, the supreme deity in Greek mythology. Terpander is recognized as the father of Greek classical music and lyrical poetry. His lyre, the kithara, had an increased number of strings — seven instead of four — and this revolutionized seventh-century music. Terpander won a prize for music with this instrument at the twenty-sixth Olympiad, held in Sparta.

The Blessing of God
rest upon all those who have been kind to us,
have cared for us, have worked for us, have served us,
and have shared our bread with us at this table.
Our merciful God,
reward all of them in your own way.
For yours is the glory and honor forever.
Amen.

— Saint Cyril (AD 850)

The Christian church in Egypt traces its origins to Saint Mark. Surnamed the Pillar of Faith, Cyril was the twenty-fourth pope of the Coptic Orthodox Church, the most brilliant theologian of the Alexandrian tradition, and one of the greatest figures in early Christian literature. After having served as archdeacon to Pope Theophilos, his uncle, he was enthroned as pope of Alexandria, the second pope in the empire.

Cyril's works reveal him as a pastor of apostolic zeal. He wrote treatises that clarified the doctrines of the Trinity and the Incarnation. He was declared a doctor of the church by Pope Leo XIII in 1882. The principal fame of Saint Cyril rests upon his defense of Catholic doctrine against the heretic Nestorius. Cyril taught that Christ was a perfect man, that the one Christ has two perfect and distinct natures, divine and human.

Prayer 20

God who invites us always to spiritual delights,
give blessing over your gifts so that we might deserve
to partake in the blessed things which ought to be
    added to your name.

Let your gifts refresh us, Lord,
and let your grace comfort us.

               — Early Christian grace (sixth century)

Graces for meals appear in the Gelasianum Sacramentarium, *the oldest extant altar book used in the Roman Catholic rite. The book documents the early practice of table prayers among Christians, and it contains the priest's part in the liturgy celebrating the Eucharist. The word* Eucharist *comes from the Greek* eucharistia, *which means "thanks giving." The Eucharist, Holy Communion, and the Lord's Supper are all fulfillment of Jesus' commandment in the New Testament to do in memory of him what he did at his Last Supper. Jesus "gave thanks" before sharing with his disciples the bread and wine that he declared to be his body and his blood.*

    The early Christian grace shown above originated in Charlemagne's request of Pope Hadrian to provide an authentic Roman sacramentary for use throughout the empire. In 785–786, the pope sent the emperor the Sacramentarium Hadrianum — *a version of the Gregorian Sacramentary intended for papal use — which he had adapted for the Carolingian empire.*

Prayer 21

Lord Christ, we pray thy mercy on our table spread,
And what thy gentle hands have given thy men
Let it by thee be blessed: whate'er we have
Came from thy lavish heart and gentle hand,
And all that's good is thine, for thou art good.
And ye that eat, give thanks for it to Christ,
And let the words ye utter be only peace,
For Christ loved peace: it was himself that said,
Peace I give unto you, my peace I leave with you.
Grant that our own may be a generous hand
Breaking the bread for all poor men, sharing the food.
Christ shall receive the bread thou gavest his poor,
And shall not tarry to give thee reward.

— Alcuin of York (734–804)

Alcuin, also known as Flaccis Albinus Alcuinus, was a medieval Christian scholar and teacher from York, England, who became the leading advisor on ecclesiastical and educational affairs in the court of Charlemagne. After having met the king of France while in Rome to petition the pope for official confirmation of York's status as an archbishopric, Alcuin was persuaded to join Charles's court. He was welcomed at the Palace School of Charlemagne, where the royal children were educated, mostly in manners and the ways of the court.

Alcuin revolutionized the educational standards of the Palace School, introducing Charlemagne to the liberal arts and creating an atmosphere of scholarship so renowned that the Palace School became known as the "school of Master Albinus." A prolific liturgical writer, he invented a handwriting style known as Caroline minuscule, which used both lowercase and uppercase letters, improving the readability of books over time through roman type.

Prayer 22

Creator Spirit, by whose aid
The world's foundations first were laid,
Come, visit every pious mind.
Come, pour thy joy on human kind.

— Medieval Latin hymn (seventh century)

This medieval Latin hymn, or Gregorian chant, "Veni, Creator Spiritus," which is ascribed to Gregory the Great or Hrabanus Maurus (seventh century), was translated by the English poet John Dryden (1631–1700). The hymn has spawned many versions, and of these Dryden's is the best known.

The Gregorian chant, the central tradition of Western Catholic music, is characterized by its well-known unaccompanied monophonic sound and is sung in precise musical modes or intervals. The Gregorian chant supplanted the other plainchant traditions of the Christian West to become the official music of the Roman Catholic liturgy.

Prayer 23

Wheresoe'er I turn mine eyes
Around on earth or toward the skies,
I see Thee in the starry field,
I see Thee in the harvest's yield,
In every breath, in every sound,
An echo of thy name is found.
The blade of grass, the simple flower,
Bear witness to Thy matchless pow'r.
My every thought, Eternal God of Heaven,
Ascends to Thee, to who all praise be given.

— Abraham ibn Ezra (1092–1167)

This prayer comes from Ibn Ezra's poem "God Everywhere." A Judaic scholar and biblical commentator, Ibn Ezra was one of the most distinguished Jewish men of letters of the Middle Ages. The great editions of the Hebrew Bible with rabbinical notations include commentaries by Ibn Ezra on many books of the Bible (Daniel, Isaiah, Proverbs, Job, and Esther, among others). His chief work is his commentary on the Torah. He became a preacher among the Jews of Christian Europe, who were unacquainted with Arabic.

Ibn Ezra led the life of a wandering teacher for thirty years and was a scholarly master of philosophy, poetry, science, and astronomy. The Abenezra Crater on the moon was named in his honor. His poetry is among the most sublime from the Middle Ages and has eternal spiritual power and beauty.

I am the one whose praise echoes on high.
I adorn all the earth.
I am the breeze that nurtures all things green.
I encourage blossoms to flourish with ripening fruits.
I am led by the spirit to feed the purest streams.
I am the rain coming from the dew
that causes the grasses to laugh with the joy of life.
I am the yearning for good.

— Hildegard of Bingen (1098–1179)

Hildegard was born into a family of nobles in the service of the counts of Sponheim, relatives of the Hohenstaufens, a dynasty of German kings. She was a German abbess and magistra of the community at Bingen on the Rhine. Hildegard reported having visions, and in response to a prophetic call from God, who demanded of her, "Write what you see," she began an account of her twenty-six mystical visions.

One of the most original intellects of medieval Europe, Hildegard was not only a prolific writer but also a mystic, a monastic leader, and a composer. Scholarly interest in women of the medieval church has led to interest in Hildegard — and particularly her music. Eighty of her compositions have survived, one of the largest repertoires of medieval compositions. You can hear an early oratorio for women's voices by Hildegard of Bingen, "O Virtus Sapientiae," in MP3 format at http://humanneuro.physiol.umu.se/GW/5mp3/O_Virtus_Sapien tiae5.mp3.

Praised be my Lord for our Mother the Earth,
which sustains us and keeps us and brings forth diverse
    fruits,
And flowers of many colors — and grass.

— Saint Francis of Assisi (1181–1226)

This prayer comes from The Canticle of the Creatures. *Saint Francis of Assisi was founder of the Franciscan Order. He spent most of his time alone, contemplating life and asking God for enlightenment. In his meditations, he had mystical experiences. On one occasion, while praying before a cross with the icon of Christ crucified, Francis witnessed Jesus on the cross come alive and say to him three times, "Francis, Francis, go and repair My house which, as you can see, is falling into ruins." At another time, Francis listened to a sermon on Matthew 10:9, in which Christ tells his followers to go forth and proclaim that the Kingdom of Heaven is upon them. He also tells them to take no money with them, not even a walking stick or shoes for the road. The sermon inspired Francis to devote himself to a life of apostolic poverty.*

In Rome, Francis sought permission from Pope Innocent III to found a new religious order, but the Pope refused. However, Innocent saw in a dream that the church was crumbling and a poor man was holding it up. He recognized the man in his dream as Francis and changed his mind about the request, validating the Franciscan Order the following day. Saint Francis is credited with setting up the first presepio, *or* crèche, *celebrating Christmas. In the* crèche, *he used real animals to create a living scenario so that worshippers could contemplate the birth of the baby Jesus in a direct way. In 1224 Francis received the stigmata, the five wounds of Christ, when he saw a vision of a seraph, a six-winged angel on a cross, who gave him the "gift" of Christ's five wounds. This is the first known account of a mortal acolyte receiving the stigmata.*

The smel of new breade is comfortable to the heade and to the herte.

— Middle English prayer (circa 1400)

Bread is one of the oldest prepared foods, dating back to the Neolithic era, and is a staple food of European, Middle Eastern, and Indian cultures. It is also a metaphor for salvation and for God, as in the expression "bread of life." The Israelites ate a flatbread called matzoh as they fled Egypt; they had no time for dough to rise as they escaped into the desert. Matzoh is still made of plain flour and water, and it is not allowed to ferment or rise before it is baked. The result is a flat, crispy, crackerlike bread. Manna was the food miraculously produced for the Israelites in the desert, according to the book of Exodus. The word manna *also refers to any divine or spiritual nourishment.*

Bread is more than just food. When friends "break bread," they share more than just a meal: they come together in spirit as well as body. The Middle English blessing above was spoken during the period between the Norman invasion (1066) and the beginning of the fifteenth century. Similar language can be found in The Canterbury Tales, *the story of thirty pilgrims who travel to Canterbury, England, written by Geoffrey Chaucer between 1387 and 1400.*

49

As for the leaves, that in the garden bloom,
my love for them is great, as is the good death
by the eternal hand that tends them all.

— Dante Alighieri (1265–1321)

This prayer comes from Canto XXVI of the Florentine poet Dante Alighieri's La Divina Commedia *(The Divine Comedy), which is considered one of the greatest literary works produced during the Middle Ages. The name* Dante *is synonymous with that of his beloved Beatrice, a young girl he fell madly in love with and immortalized in his works.* The Divine Comedy *narrates Dante's journey though hell, purgatory, and paradise. He is initially guided by the poet Virgil, who cannot enter paradise because he is a pagan. At that point, Beatrice, Dante's ideal woman, becomes Dante's guide. Dante loves God, and he finally comes to release his love and make that leap of faith (having been guided back to his faith by Virgil) when he sees Beatrice on the other side of the Great Divide.*

The "garden" in paradise evokes the Garden of Eden, where the tree of life blooms and offers an afterlife of eternal happiness. The Garden of Eden represents not a geographical place but rather a concept of eternal happiness, in which humankind would live off God's bounty, for which they would be eternally thankful. Thus did Dante emerge from his monumental depression and regain his belief in God.

Be a gardener,
dig a ditch,
toil and sweat,
and turn the earth upside down
and seek the deepness
and water the plants in time.
Continue this labor
and make sweet floods to run
and noble and abundant fruits
to spring.
Take this food and drink
and carry it to God
as your true worship.

— Julian of Norwich (circa 1373)

In 1373, at age thirty, the English mystic and religious writer Julian of Norwich, also known as Mother Juliana, had sixteen visions of Jesus, which she glorified in her Revelations of Divine Love. *This is believed to be the first book written by a woman in the English language. Julian was an anchoress, who, in this early Christian medieval time, withdrew from secular society to lead an intensely prayer-oriented life. Her visions were the source of her work. Over a twenty-year period, she explored her personal theology and contemplated and embraced the mystery of God's love, speaking of it in terms of optimism and joy, as opposed to obedience and duty.*

Christ, the gladdener of all, without whom nothing is sweet or pleasant, bless, we beg of you, the food and drink of your servants, which you have now provided for our bodily sustenance; and grant that we may use these gifts to praise you, and may enjoy them with grateful hearts; grant too that, just as our body is nurtured by bodily foods, so too our mind may feed on the spiritual nourishment of your Word, through you our Lord.

— From the services at Christ's College,
University of Cambridge (1535)

This prayer was written and delivered at Christ's College one Sunday in 1535, the year after King Henry VIII dismantled the Catholic Church in England and assumed supremacy over Rome. England had embraced the Roman Catholic faith for nearly a thousand years, until this separation in 1534. Henry had decided to divorce Catherine of Aragon, as she had not produced an heir, a son, but Pope Clement refused to annul the marriage. The previous year, Henry had learned that Anne Boleyn, the woman he wanted as his wife, was pregnant with his child (Princess Elizabeth). Sir Thomas More, Lord Chancellor to Henry, refused to accept the king's claim to be supreme head of the Church of England, a decision that led to his execution as a traitor. Henry appointed Thomas Cranmer as bishop of Canterbury, who summarily granted the divorce. The pope responded to the remarriage by excommunicating both Henry and Cranmer. Henry manipulated Parliament to make him "supreme head on earth of the Church of England."

Christ's College, part of the University of Cambridge, is one of the oldest universities in the world.

And now, O friends,
hear the dream of a word:
Each spring gives us life,
the golden ear of corn refreshes us,
the tender ear of corn becomes a necklace for us.
We know that the hearts of our friends are true.

— Nahuatl prayer (sixteenth century)

This exquisite prayer and food blessing composed by native people of Mexico is suffused with sublime imagery of and thankfulness for the bounty of the earth, and it illustrates the veneration of corn. Imagine: genetic evidence indicates that maize domestication occurred nine thousand years ago in central Mexico. After the European contact with the Americas in the fifteenth and sixteenth centuries, corn spread throughout the world.

The word corn *is a shortened form of the term* Indian corn, *that is, the Indian grain. Nahuatl is the language of the ancient Aztec empire and is still spoken today in Mexico. The Aztecs were a pre-Columbian Mesoamerican people of central Mexico who built an extensive empire, and who called themselves Mexicas. The Spanish conquest led by Hernán Cortés initiated the displacement of Nahuatl by the Spanish language, and, over subsequent centuries, Nahuatl has become obscure.*

Prayer 31

O heavenly Father, you have filled the world
with beauty and provided us in abundance.
Open your eyes to behold
your gracious hand in all your works;
that rejoicing in your whole creation,
we may learn to serve you with gladness.

— Book of Common Prayer (sixteenth century)

Prayer 32

Almighty God, whose loving
hand hath given us all that we possess:
Give us also grace to honor thee with our substance,
remembering the account we must one day give
as faithful stewards of thy bounty;
for the sake of Jesus Christ our Lord.

— Book of Common Prayer (eighteenth century)

The Book of Common Prayer, the foundational prayer book used in both Anglican and Episcopalian churches, is one of the major works of English literature. It has exerted enormous influence on the religious and literary lives of all who speak the English language. The Book of Common Prayer was the first complete book of devotions created by the clergy in the common language of the people, enabling them, for the first time, to participate actively in worship.

First published in 1549, it was revised several times, most significantly in 1662, when Parliament made the use of the book compulsory for all rites and ceremonies in services conducted in the Church of England. The book was the prime instrument of the Protestant Reformation, undertaken to reform the Catholic Church. Parliament's Act of Uniformity in 1872 further prescribed the form of additional prayers, sacraments, and rites. The Book of Common Prayer has gone through a number of editions, not only in England, where it originated, but also in all churches of the Anglican Communion, including the Episcopal Church in the United States and the Churches of England, Scotland, Wales, Canada, Congo, Japan, Australia, and others.

Prayer 33

This ritual is one.
This food is one.
We who offer the food are one.
The fire of hunger is also one.
All action is one.
We who understand this are one.

— Ancient Hindu blessing said before meals (2500–600 BC)

Prayer 34

The cow from whom all plenty flows,
Obedient to her saintly lord,
Viands to suit each taste outpoured.
Honey she gave, and roasted grain,
Mead sweet with flowers, and sugar-cane.
Each beverage of flavor rare,
And food of every sort, were there:
Hills of hot rice, and sweetened cakes,
And curdled milk, and soup in lakes.
Vast beakers flowing to the brim
With sugared drink prepared for him;
And dainty sweetmeats, deftly made,
Before the hermit's guests were laid.

— Ancient Hindu poem (2500–600 BC)

Prayer 35

This night I hold an old accustom'd feast,
Whereto I have invited many a guest,
Such as I love; and you among them the store,
One more, most welcome, makes my number more.

— William Shakespeare (1564–1616),
Romeo and Juliet, act 1, scene 2, line 20

Prayer 36

O Lord, that lends me life,
Lend me a heart replete with thankfulness.

— William Shakespeare (1564–1616),
The Second Part of *King Henry VI*, act 1, scene 1, lines 19–20

Prayer 35 refers to an invitation to a masked ball, where Romeo sees and instantly falls in love with Juliet. It is also a perfect food blessing in that it celebrates friendship and welcoming a guest to the table with the distinct honor that, among the many guests present, this guest is the most welcome. Lovely thought. Prayer 36 makes a fine table grace as it is a humble praise to God that expresses thankfulness for life and its bounty. Shakespeare is regarded as the greatest writer in the English language. He is also the most-quoted author ever. He wrote 38 plays, 154 sonnets, and many other poems.

Prayer, the Church's banquet, Angels' age,
    God's breath in man returning to his birth,
The soul in paraphrase, heart in pilgrimage,
    The Christian plummet, sounding heaven and
    earth;
Engine against the Almighty, sinner's tower,
    Reversed thunder, Christ-side-piercing spear,
The six-days' world transposing in an hour,
    A kind of tune, which all things hear and
    fear;
Softness and peace, and joy, and love,
    and bliss,
    Exalted manna, gladness of the best,
    Heaven in ordinary, man well drest,
The milky way, the bird of Paradise,
    Church-bells beyond the stars heard,
    The soul's blood,
    The land of spices; something understood.

— George Herbert (1593–1633)

Prayer 38

To all else thou hast given us, O Lord,
we ask for but one thing more:
Give us
grateful hearts.

— George Herbert (1593–1633)

A clergyman in the Church of England, George Herbert wrote religious poems characterized by precise language and by humility. Many of his poems have been used as hymns and set to music by famed composers. Herbert was elected a major fellow of Trinity College at the University of Cambridge. In 1618 he was appointed Reader in Rhetoric at the university, and in 1620 he was elected public orator there, serving until 1628. The latter was a post conferring dignity and even some authority: its incumbent was called on to express, in the florid Latin of the day, the sentiments of the university on public occasions. Herbert was known as "Holy Mr. Herbert" around the countryside.

Love bade me
Welcome: yet my soul drew back,
Guiltie of dust and sinne.
But quick-ey'd Love, observing me grow slack
From my first entrance in,
Drew nearer to me, sweetly questioning,
If I lack'd anything.

A guest, I answer'd, worthy to be here:
Love said, You shall be he.
I, the unkinde, ungratefull? Ah my deare,
I cannot look on thee.
Love took my hand, and smiling did reply,
Who made the eyes but I?

Truth Lord, but I have marr'd them: let my shame
Go where it doth deserve.
And know you not, sayes Love, who bore the blame?
My deare, then I will serve.
You must sit down, sayes Love, and taste my meat:
So I did sit and eat.

— George Herbert (1593–1633)

This poem is about the Lord's Supper and, more generally, about Christian life. Herbert pictures Christ as an innkeeper who welcomes a weary, dejected traveler. Deeply aware of his guilt and lack of gratitude, the guest finds it difficult to accept such generous hospitality. But the innkeeper reminds him that the Creator who made all our human gifts, such as our eyes, is also the Savior who can redeem them no matter how badly we have "marr'd" them. The traveler still wants to "bring something to the table," as we say, so he offers to serve the innkeeper. No, says the innkeeper, the traveler must sit down and enjoy the meal. The table at the Lord's Supper, and by extension Christian life, is one table where we are never hosts but always guests. We are unconditionally loved and encouraged to feast, no matter how unworthy we feel. For an example of music of the period, listen to "My Thoughts Are Winged with Hope," by John Dowland (1562–1626) at http://www.luminarium.org/sevenlit/herbert/.

Let us, with a gladsome mind,
Praise the Lord, for He is kind;
For His mercies still endure,
Ever faithful, ever sure.

All things living
He doth feed,
His full hand supplied their need.

Let us with a gladsome mind
Praise the Lord, for He is kind.

— John Milton (1609–1674)

This poem is often sung as a hymn, with music by Johann Sebastian Bach. Milton is considered to be among the most learned of all English poets. A graduate of Christ's College at the University of Cambridge, he was a true intellect with full command of theology, philosophy, history, and literature. Milton had a Puritan upbringing and embraced the religious perspective that sought the reform of liturgy and theology away from Catholicism. His epic work, Paradise Lost, *is a narrative poem based upon scripture about the Fall of Man and the expulsion of Adam and Eve from the Garden of Eden. Milton's narrative has many wonderful passages about the bounty of the earth, such as that of an angel, who "Beholding shall confess that here on Earth God hath dispenst his bounties as in Heav'n."*

Milton was blind when he wrote Paradise Lost, *and he completed it with the help of friends. The above poem is not from* Paradise Lost, *but it reiterates his love of God and belief that we must praise the Lord for providing us with both spiritual and physical food.*

Our Father, who art in heaven,
hallowed be thy name.
Thy kingdom come;
thy will be done on earth as it is in heaven.
Give us this day our daily bread;
and forgive us our trespasses
as we forgive those who trespass against us;
and lead us not into temptation,
but deliver us from evil.

— The Lord's Prayer, Traditional Matthean Version of the
Bible, Roman Catholic, Matthew 6:9–13 (circa AD 60–90)

*This essential Christian prayer is also found in Luke 11:2–4. No other
example of the written word has a hold upon humankind like the few brief
sentences of the Lord's Prayer, which sums up the teachings of Jesus. This
prayer is recited by every Christian church, in every service, from baptism to burial. In the Lord's Prayer there are six petitions: three for God's
glory, three for our needs. With these words, we as petitioners ask God
to help us recognize all the blessings he showers on us and thank Him for
these blessings, which are all that we need in this life.*

*During the Middle Ages, this prayer was always said in Latin, and
it was then known as the Pater Noster (Our Father). The Roman
Catholic version usually omits the doxology "For Thine is the kingdom,
power, and glory, forever and ever." This addition was imposed in England during the reign of Henry VIII, and it appears in the 1549 and
1552 editions of the Book of Common Prayer, which became widely popular during the reign of Elizabeth I of England, around 1580.*

Prayer 42

Our Father, which art in heaven, Hallowed be thy
 Name.
Thy kingdom come. Thy will be done, in earth as it is
 in heaven.
Give us this day our daily bread.
And forgive us our trespasses,
As we forgive them that trespass against us.
And lead us not into temptation;
But deliver us from evil:
For thine is the kingdom, the power, and the glory,
For ever and ever. Amen.

— Anglican Book of Prayer (1662)

The Lord's Prayer through the ages:

Oure fader that art in heuenis halowid be thi name...

— Early Middle English Bible (1100–1300)

Our Father which art in heaven, hallowed be thy name.

— Book of Common Prayer (1599)

Our father which art in heauen, hallowed be thy name.
Thy kingdome come. Thy will be done, in earth, as it
 is in heauen.

Giue vs this day our daily bread.

And forgiue vs our debts, as we forgiue our debters.

And lead vs not into temptation, but deliuer vs from
   euill:

For thine is the kingdome, and the power, and the
   glory,

for euer, Amen.

— King James Version of the Bible (1611; original language)

Prayer 43

Jesus then took the loaves,

and when he had given thanks,

he distributed them to those who were seated,

so also the fish,

as much as they wanted.

                    — John 6:11, Bible, Revised Standard Version

Prayer 44

Praise God, from whom all blessings flow,
Praise Him, all creatures here below,
Praise Him above, ye heavenly host,
Praise Father, Son, and Holy Ghost. Amen.

— Christian doxology

Prayer 45

Glory to the Father and to the Son
and to the Holy Spirit;
as it was in the beginning is now
and shall be for ever. Amen.

— Anglican doxology

Prayer 46

Through him, with him, in him, in the unity of the
    Holy Spirit;
all glory and honor is yours, almighty Father, forever
    and ever. Amen.

— Roman Catholic doxology

*These hymns of praise to God are examples of Christian doxology
(from the Greek word* doxa, *meaning "glory"). A doxology is a short
hymn of praise to God in Christian worship often appearing at the end
of hymns and Psalms. Early Christian rites adopted from the synagogue
the custom of ending each prayer with a doxa. "Gloria Patri et Spiritu
Sancto" is known as the little doxology, the great doxology being "Gloria in Excelsis Deo." Judaism also employs doxological forms. The little doxology, which is addressed to the Trinity, is the most common
doxology used by Catholics and many Protestant religions. It is also
known as the "Gloria Patri," so named for its first two words in Latin.*

Prayer 47

One does not live by bread alone,
but by every word that comes
from the mouth of God.

— Matthew 4:4, Bible,
New Revised Standard Version

Prayer 48

O Lord,
I will give thanks unto thee for ever.

— Psalm 30:12, Bible, American Standard Version

For the Lord your God is bringing you into a good
    land,
a land of flowing streams, with springs and under-
    ground waters welling up in valleys and hills,
a land of wheat and barley, of vines and fig trees and
    pomegranates,
a land of olive trees and honey, a land where you may
    eat bread without scarcity,
where you will lack nothing, a land whose stones are
    iron
and from whose hills you may mine copper.

You shall eat your fill and bless the Lord your God
for the good land he has given you.

— Deuteronomy 8:7–10, Bible,
New Revised Standard Version

Deuteronomy is the fifth book of the Hebrew Bible, which Jews call the Tanakh and Christians call the Old Testament. Deuteronomy consists chiefly of discourses delivered by Moses to his people at the end of his life. These describe, in some of the most beautiful biblical language, the gifts of God and how humankind should appreciate them and serve the Lord. Deuteronomy is one book that contains the well-known reminder "not by bread alone doth man live." It also charges humankind to keep the Lord's commandments, saying that he will lead us out of the wilderness to the land of milk and honey, and that we will enjoy the abundance of all things. Cast your thoughts back to biblical times and reread these inspiring words within this context.

Prayer 50

Cast thy bread upon the waters:
for thou shalt find it after many days.

— Ecclesiastes 11:1, Bible,
American Standard Version

Ecclesiastes exhorts us to undertake works of mercy, telling us we have an obligation to do good. The water metaphor has many interpretations, and its context is a discussion of benevolence. The lesson here is to be a benevolent person, because we never know when we might be in need of benevolence ourselves. The metaphor would have been familiar to people of the time in which it was written. It derives from the custom of sowing seed by casting it from boats into overflowing rivers or onto marshy ground. When the waters recede, the grain will lie deep in the soil and spring up, a life-saving crop. As another possible interpretation, the image of water may also be intended to represent people, many people, who might be the recipients of our benevolent efforts, and who in time will show benevolence to us when we need it.

Prayer 51

Praised are You, Lord our God, King of the universe,
for all the nourishment and produce of the field,
for the lovely and spacious land
which You gave to our fathers as a heritage
to eat of its fruit and enjoy its good gifts.
Have mercy, Lord our God,
on Your people Israel, on Your altar and Your shrine.
Speedily rebuild the holy city of Jerusalem.
Bring us there and gladden us with the restoration of
      our land.
May we eat of its fruit and enjoy its good gifts.
May we bless You for it in holiness and purity.

— Ancient Jewish blessing

Prayer 52

Whether therefore ye eat,
or drink, or whatsoever ye do,
do all to the glory of God.

— 1 Corinthians 10:31, Bible,
King James Version

But when you give a feast, invite the poor,
the maimed, the lame, the blind,
and you will be blessed,
because they cannot repay you.
You will be repaid at the resurrection of the just.

— Luke 14:13–14, Bible,
Revised Standard Version

Prayer 54

From the sky you send rain on the hills,
and the earth is filled with your blessings.
You make the grass grow for the cattle
and plants for man to use
so that he can grow his crops
and produce wine to make him happy,
olive oil to make him cheerful,
and bread to give him strength.

— Psalm 104:13–15, Hebrew Bible,
Today's English Version

Prayer 55

Blessed are you, Lord, our God, King of the universe,
who brings forth bread from the earth.

*Barukh ata Adonai Eloheinu melekh ha olam, ha motzi
lehem min ha aretz.*

— Birkat Hazan (prayer before eating bread)

This prayer is from the Torah. The Hebrew word for law is Torah, *and
the Torah is the first five books of the Hebrew Bible, composed between
220 BC and AD 100. The Torah and the Talmud, the compilation of Judaism's Oral Law, are the foundation for prayers before taking food.
The Birkat Hazan is said before eating bread, or matzah, made from
wheat, barley rye, oats, or spelt.*

Prayer 56

Let the people praise thee, O God:
    let all people praise thee.
Then shall the earth bring forth the increase:
    and God, even our own God,
    shall give us his blessing.
God shall bless us:
    and all the ends of the world
    shall fear him.

— Psalm 67, Hebrew Bible

72

I sent out invitations
To summon guests.
I collected together all my friends.
Loud talk
And ample feasting:
Discussion of philosophy,
Investigation of subtleties.
Tongues loosened
And minds at one.
Hearts refreshed
By discharge of emotion!

— Ch'eng-kung Sui (died AD 273)

China is the oldest surviving civilization in the world. This extraordinary ancient poem personifies hospitality and a gathering of friends for a feast and intelligent conversation. This poem is as inspiring today as when it was written over seventeen hundred years ago. The thoughts are a sublime expression of the pleasure of sharing and enjoying life through the entertainment of guests with warmth and goodwill. At this meal, tongues would have been loosened by warmed alcoholic beverages.

In the Name of Allah!
Bi Ismillahi!
  (before eating)
Thanks to Allah, Master of both worlds!
  (this and the afterworld)
Al Hamdu Lillaahi Rabbil 'Aalamin!
  (after eating)

— Traditional Muslim prayer

Muslims believe in Islam, a monotheistic religion based on the teachings of Muhammad, a seventh-century religious figure. Muhammad received revelations from God, and these revelations, known collectively as the Koran (Quran), were recorded by his followers around AD 650. The essential creed of Islam is expressed in the following: "I testify that there is none worthy of worship except God, and I testify that Muhammad is the Messenger of God" ('ašhadu 'al-lā ilāha illā-llāh, wa 'ašhadu 'anna muḥammadan rasūlu-llāh). The two main branches of Islam are Shia and Sunni; the latter is the largest.

Devout Muslims say salat, *or obligatory, prayers five times each day while facing Mecca and the Sacred Mosque. Inside a large open space within the mosque stands the Kaaba, a sacred forty-nine-foot-tall cubical building, which is the focal point for prayer (analogous to the Christian cross). Devotees who make a pilgrimage to Mecca walk around the Kaaba while praying.* Halal *foods are those that Islamic rituals and laws permit Muslims to eat. The word is analogous to* kosher, *a term used in the Jewish faith. Muhammad said, "Mention Allah's name on it and eat."*

Lord of Lords, Creator of all things,
    God of all things, God over all gods,
    God of sun and rain,
    You created the earth with a thought
    and us with your breath.

Lord, we brought in the harvest.
The rain watered the earth, the sun drew cassava and
    corn out of the clay.
Your mercy showered blessing after blessing over our
    country.
Creeks grew into rivers; swamps became lakes.
Healthy fat cows graze on the green sea of the savanna.
The rain smoothed out the clay walls, the mosquitoes
    drowned in the high waters.

Lord, the yam is fat like meat, the cassava melts on the
    tongue, oranges burst in their peels, dazzling and
    bright.

Lord, nature gives thanks, Your creatures give thanks.
Your praise rises in us like the great river.

                      — West African prayer

Heavenly Father
Bless this food
Make it holy
Let no impurity or greed defile it
The food comes from thee
It is for thy temple
Spiritualize it
We are the petals of thy manifestation
But thou art the flower
Its life, beauty, and loveliness
Permeate our souls with the fragrance of thy presence
OM — peace — amen.

— Hindu prayer

Aum (OM) is the most sacred symbol in Hindu dharma. Aum is the sound of the infinite. It is composed of three Sanskrit letters: the letter A represents creation, the letter U refers to the god Vishnu, and the M produces resonance in the nasal cavity when sounded with the mouth closed. The three letters also indicate three planes of existence, heaven (swarga), earth (martya), and the netherworld (patala). Liberation from the world does not mean abandoning the world but merging into the world and beyond, becoming the all, a state called nirvana. The doctrine of karma (karmavada) is based upon the theory of cause and effect.

Puja, a Sanskrit word meaning reverence or worship, is a religious ritual that Hindus perform twice a day. Puja rites are performed before eating. Fruits and other foods accompanied by flowers are allowed as offerings to God.

Thank You, Lord.

Wen na régé.

— Prayer from Burkina Faso, West Africa

*The name Burkina Faso comes from Mooré and Jula root words mean-
ing "the land of upright and honest men." Approximately 50 percent
of the population of this nation is Muslim and 30 percent is Christian.
The balance consists of devotees to traditional African animist religions
who have resisted Islam and Christianity. Many Christians and Muslims incorporate elements of animism into their religious practices too.
The Mossi, a rural people who practice animism, have retained the use
of traditional tribal masks and figures. The masks invoke protective
totemic spirits of the clan and ancestors. During rituals, the spirits are im-
plored to bring an abundant rainy season and to provide for the people's
well-being throughout the coming year. In this country of droughts, crops
often fail or are poor, and often there is not sufficient grain to sustain
the villagers through the "hungry season" until the next harvest.*

*The Burkina Faso Embassy provided this food blessing. You can hear
a sample of ceremonial music from Burkina Faso at http://encarta.msn
.com/media_461563645/Traditional_Fulani_Music_of_Benin.html.*

The bread is not our food.
What feeds us in the bread is God's eternal Word,
is spirit and is life.

— Angelus Silesius (1624–1677)

A German mystic and poet of the Counter-Reformation, also known as the Catholic Deformation, Angelus Silesius was baptized Johannes Scheffler and was born in the province of Silesia, now within the borders of Poland. After the end of the Thirty Years' War in 1646, the Hapsburgs greatly encouraged Catholicism and succeeded in reconverting to Catholicism about 60 percent of the population of Silesia. Silesius was at the forefront of this conversion. In 1653, he had converted to Catholicism from Lutheranism, and he spent the rest of his life trying to reconvert the people of Silesia. He is known mainly for his mystical poetry, which primarily took the form of Alexandrines, simple rhymed couplets with a specific linguistic sound pattern (compare the rhythm of lines 1 and 3 above). His writing many seem naive, but the depth of feeling cannot be denied, and his works approach the depth of haiku and other short mystical poetry from around the world.

Prayer 63

Lord of the harvest, hear
    Thy needy servants cry;
Answer our faith's effectual prayer,
    And all our wants supply.

On thee we humbly wait,
    Our wants are in thy view:
The harvest truly, Lord, is great,
    The laborers are few.

— Charles Wesley (1707–1788)

Charles Wesley, the "sweet singer of Methodism," was both a preacher and the most gifted and prolific of all English hymn writers. Along with his older brother, John Wesley, he initially preached around the country and formed local societies, which eventually became the Methodist Church. His sixty-five hundred hymns, seventeen years of itinerant preaching, and superintendence of the London societies make him a major figure in the creation of the Methodist movement. His love for the Church of England was largely responsible for the Anglican tradition within Methodism. In 1780, Wesley published his Collection of Hymns for the Use of the People Called Methodists, *in which some of the hymns are attributed to both John and Charles Wesley. This collection remains the standard Methodist hymnal. Wesley's commitment to God is expressed in such hymns as "Hark! The Herald Angels Sing," "Love Divine," and "Christ the Lord Is Risen Today."*

Prayer 64

O God Our Father,
the foundation of all goodness,
who has been gracious to us,
not only in the year that is past
but throughout all the years of our lives;
we give you thanks for your loving kindness
which has filled our days
and brought us to this time and place.

— John Wesley (1703–1791)

Prayer 65

Be present at our table, Lord,
Be here and everywhere adored.
Thy creatures bless, and grant that we
May feast in Paradise with Thee.

— John Wesley (1703–1791)

John Wesley and his brother, Charles Wesley (see prayer 63), founded the Methodist Church in Great Britain (England, Scotland, Wales) during the eighteenth century. Methodism began as a movement within the Church of England that focused on avid Bible study. Originally, it appealed especially to workers and poor farmers. Because many local parish churches were closed to him, Wesley pioneered open-air preaching to common people in the fields. Unable to reach people from established church pulpits, and unwilling to let them perish in their sins, he sought them out in the open countryside. As a result, this feature of Methodism, to which it largely owed its success, was adopted by Wesley in answer to a necessity. He also pioneered lay preaching, in which men and women who were not ordained were permitted to preach and do pastoral work.

The famous "Holy Club" was formed by John's younger brother, Charles Wesley, and some fellow students. The club met to read, study scripture, and undergo rigorous self-examination of their Christian lives. In 1732, the term Methodists *was first used to describe these men as it reflected the method and order in their lives. The Wesleys and the Methodists were persecuted by Anglican clergymen and magistrates. Prayer 65 is often sung to the hymn "Praise God from Whom All Blessings Flow."*

Prayer 66

Bless us O Lord, for these gifts
we are about to receive from your bounty.

— Traditional Christian grace (nineteenth century)

Prayer 67

Some hae meat and canna eat,
And some wad eat that want it;
But we hae meat and we can eat,
And sae the Lord be thankit.

— Robert Burns (1759–1796),
"The Selkirk Grace"

A Scottish farmer, a prolific poet, and a songwriter, Robert Burns was considered a cultural icon and was the National Poet of Scotland. "The Selkirk Grace" is universally attributed to Burns, but historians point out that this food blessing was already in use in his time. It is therefore also referred to as "A Poet's Grace."

"The Selkirk Grace" speaks of Selkirk, a fabled town in the Scottish Borders region possessed of traditions, spirit, and history that dates back to Roman times. By making use of Scottish Gaelic, Burns brings to life the earthy reality of a language that goes back thousands of years — the language of Middle Irish (spoken from the tenth to the sixteenth centuries).

O Thou, who kindly doth provide
For ev'ry creature's want!
We bless the God of Nature wide
For all Thy goodness lent,
And if it please Thee, heavenly Guide,
May never worse be sent;
But, whether granted or denied,
Lord, bless us with content.

— Robert Burns (1759–1796)

An extemporaneous grace before dinner, this prayer was improvised by the poet at a dinner table in Dumfries in southern Scotland. Scotland is a Christian country whose national church is the Church of Scotland, known as the Kirk, a reformed Presbyterian (as opposed to Episcopal) religion based on the teachings of John Calvin and John Knox.

Prayer 69

When you rise in the morning,
give thanks for the light,
for your Life, for your Strength.
Give Thanks for your Food and for the joy of Living.
If you see no reason to give thanks,
the Fault Lies in Yourself.

— Tecumseh (1768–1813)

Tecumseh, chief of the Shawnee Nation, was greatly admired in his day and remains a towering icon for Native Americans; he is considered a national hero in Canada. Following the American Revolution, the Indian peoples were slaughtered and pushed from their homelands by white settlers. The warrior Tecumseh wanted to preserve Shawnee land and led raids against the settlers. He also allied with the British in the War of 1812. They thought so highly of his character that they commissioned him as a brigadier general. Tecumseh was known for his saintlike compassion and opposition to unnecessary killing. His intellect and morality sings out in this eloquent credo, from which I've drawn prayer 69 (emphasis mine):

> *So live your life that the fear of death can never enter your heart. Trouble no one about their religion; respect others in their view, and demand that they respect yours. Love your life, perfect your life, beautify all things in your life. Seek to make your life long and its purpose in the service of your people. Prepare a noble death song for the day when you go over the great divide. Always give a word or a sign of salute when meeting or*

passing a friend, even a stranger, when in a lonely place. Show respect to all people and grovel to none. When you arise in the morning give thanks for the food and for the joy of living. If you see no reason for giving thanks, the fault lies only in yourself. *Abuse no one and no thing, for abuse turns the wise ones to fools and robs the spirit of its vision. When it comes your time to die, be not like those whose hearts are filled with the fear of death, so that when their time comes they weep and pray for a little more time to live their lives over again in a different way. Sing your death song and die like a hero going home.*

Prayer 70

For peaceful homes, and healthful days,
For all the blessings Earth displays,
We owe Thee thankfulness and praise,
Giver of all!

— Christopher Wadsworth, Anglican bishop (1807–1885)

Prayer 71

For each new morning with its light,
For rest and shelter of the night,
For health and food,
For love and friends,
For everything Thy goodness sends.

— Ralph Waldo Emerson (1803–1882)

Emerson was a prolific American essayist and poet who graduated from Harvard Divinity School in 1829 and became a Unitarian minister. He was among a group of leading intellectuals in the Boston area who founded Transcendentalism, a philosophy that protested the general state of society and culture and, in particular, challenged the Unitarian Congregational belief in the oneness of God (which rejected the Trinity) and the belief that Jesus was a moral man but not God. Emerson and friends held that humankind's ultimate nature "transcends" the physical and is realized through individual intuition, rather than through established religions. In his belief that God is immanent in each person and in nature, he asserted that intuition was the source of knowledge enabling people to reject religion and rely on their individuality. Within the individual was the soul of the whole world. Emerson's essay "Self-Reliance" is among his most famous.

A circle of friends is a blessed thing.
Sweet is the breaking of bread with friends.
For the honor of their presence at our board
We are deeply grateful, Lord.

Thanks be to Thee for friendship shared,
Thanks be to Thee for food prepared.
Bless Thou the cup; bless Thou the bread;
Thy blessing rest upon each head.

— Walter Rauschenbusch (1861–1918)

Walter Rauschenbusch was an American Baptist minister who "wanted to do hard work for God," a calling he fulfilled as a pastor in Hell's Kitchen in New York City. Life in the slums thrust in his face the need of the working poor for better health care and better food, among other things. A champion of social reform, he founded the nondenominational Kingdom of God to address the problems of the working poor and immigrants through the application of Christian principles to social problems, specifically poverty, alcoholism, crime, poor schools, poor hygiene, and child labor. The contemporary question of Evangelicals — "What would Jesus do?" — was the moral model for his ministry. The first line of this blessing, "A circle of friends is a blessed thing," is an exquisite statement of thanks giving.

Heap high the farmer's wintry hoard!
    Heap high the golden corn!
No richer gift has Autumn poured
    From out her lavish horn!

But let the good old crop adorn
    The hills our fathers trod;
Still let us, for His golden corn,
    Send up our thanks to God!

— John Greenleaf Whittier (1807–1892)

Prayer 74

O Brother Man, fold to thy heart thy brother;
Where pity dwells, the peace of God is there;
To worship rightly is to love each other,
Each smile a hymn, each kindly deed a prayer.

— John Greenleaf Whittier (1807–1892)

John Greenleaf Whittier was a Quaker patriot and writer and an avid Abolitionist who decried slavery. He was raised in Haverhill, Massachusetts, in a large farm family and knew the joy and rewards of the harvest, as expressed in Prayer 73, taken from his poem "The Corn-Song." He became an editor for several Boston newspapers and wrote poetry and hymns that embrace a universalist spirit. Nineteenth-century Universalists emphasized the ideas of individual piety and a zeal for "religion of the heart." They believed that a God of love would not create a person knowing that that person would be destined for eternal damnation. A bard of the common man, Whittier composed more than a hundred hymns that were deeply religious and that praised God. Prayer 74 above is taken from one of his hymns.

Come, ye thankful people,
  Come, raise the song of harvest home:
All is safely gathered in,
  Ere the winter storm begin;
God, our Maker, does provide for our wants to be
  supplied;
  Come to God's own temple, come, raise the song
  of harvest home.

All the world is God's own field,
  Fruit unto his praise to yield;
Wheat and tares together sown,
  Unto joy or sorrow grown.
First the blade, and then the ear,
  Then the full corn shall appear;
Grant, O harvest Lord, that we
  Wholesome grain and pure may be.

— Henry Alford (1810–1871)

The English poet, hymnist, and biblical scholar Henry Alford is best known as the author of the Thanksgiving hymn "Come, Ye Thankful People, Come," written in 1844, part of which appears here as prayer 75. Among scholars, he is better known for his commentary on the Greek New Testament, on which he labored for eighteen years. He had a knack for explaining things in a way that a lay audience could understand.

After many years of hard work, Alford accepted a position at Canterbury Cathedral that allowed him more time to write. His preaching style was evangelical. Formal church leaders considered him a bit radical, but his good humor and friendliness won their affection. Hear the music to the hymn "Come, Ye Thankful People, Come" at http://www.cyberhymnal.org/htm/c/o/comeytpc.htm. The music was written by Alford's contemporary, George J. Elvy of Saint George's Chapel, Windsor, England.

Prayer 76

So once a year we throng
Upon a day apart,
To praise the Lord with feast and song,
In thankfulness of heart.

— Arthur Guiterman (1871–1943)

Arthur Guiterman was born to American parents in Vienna, graduated from the College of the City of New York in 1891, served as editor of the Literary Digest *and the* Woman's Home Companion, *and co-founded the Poetry Society of America in 1910. He also published books on verse and was considered an accomplished American poet of feeling and grace.*

How beautiful and perfect are the animals!
How perfect the Earth, and the minutest thing
on it!
What is called good is perfect, and what is
called bad is just as perfect;
The vegetables and minerals are all perfect,
    and the imponderable fluids perfect.
Slowly and surely they have pass'd on to this,
    and slowly and surely they pass on.
I swear I think there is nothing but immortality.

— Walt Whitman (1819–1892)

Walt Whitman, an American Romantic poet, was an iconoclast who broke or disdained established literary conventions with his epic Leaves of Grass, *which abandoned traditional meter in favor of an irregular rhythmic freestyle structure. Whitman praised nature and our place in it, celebrating the human body and mind in a unique poetic statement. He wrote* Leaves of Grass *in response to Emerson's essay "The Poet," which pointed to the need for the United States to have its own new and unique poet to write about the new country's virtues and vices. Whitman sent Emerson his collection of poems — the collection that would become* Leaves of Grass — *and fame followed instantaneously. After Whitman's magnum opus was published, in 1855, certain of the poems prompted a firestorm of criticism by those who considered them obscene.*

Born in Huntington, Whitman left Long Island — where he is still much revered — at age twenty-two. He is buried at Camden, New Jersey, where he lived his last years. He is considered to be among the most important of all American poets.

Recall the face of the poorest
and most helpless man whom you may have seen
and ask yourself if the step you contemplate
is going to be of any use to him.
Will it restore him to a control
over his own life and destiny?
Will it lead to self rule for the hungry
and spiritually starved millions
of our fellow men?
If so, then you will find your doubts and yourself
melting away.

— Mohandas Gandhi (1869–1948)

The Indian spiritual leader Mohandas Gandhi asserted the unity of humankind under one God and preached Christian, Muslim, and Hindi ethics. He was one of the most revered souls of the twentieth century. Albert Einstein said that forthcoming generations would not even believe that such a man had walked on this planet. Gandhi focused his political activity on self-rule for the hungry and spiritually starved millions in India and on winning independence from the British. He used the absence of food — fasting and hunger strikes — as a powerful moral and political statement.

Gandhi's concept of civil disobedience was directly influenced by Henry David Thoreau's essay "On Civil Disobedience." He said that his philosophy was also based on the teachings of the Bhagavad Gita, the compassion of Buddha, and the passion of Christ for service to humankind. Later in his life when he was asked whether he was a Hindu, he replied, "Yes, I am. I am also a Christian, a Muslim, a Buddhist, and a Jew."

Prayer 79

Lord behold our family here assembled.
We thank Thee for this place in which
We dwell, for the love that unites us, for
The peace accorded us this day,
For the Health, the work, the food, and the bright
Skies that make our lives delight, for
Our friends in all parts of the earth.

Give us courage, gaiety, and the quiet mind.
Spare to us our friends, soften to us our enemies.
Bless us, if it may be, in all our innocent endeavors.
If it may not, give us the strength to encounter that
    which is to come.
May we be brave in peril, constant in tribulation, tem-
    perate in wrath,
And in all changes of fortune loyal and loving to one
    another.

— Robert Louis Stevenson (1850–1894)

Robert Louis Stevenson was a Scottish novelist, poet, and travel writer with an appetite for adventure, whose ill health prompted him to journey to distant countries in search of a climate that would comfort him. But it was love for his fiancée in San Francisco that drew him to New York and a trip across America by wagon train, which he documented in books and articles. Author of Treasure Island *and* The Strange Case of Dr. Jekyll & Mr. Hyde, *Stevenson eventually mounted a quest for health and indulged a thirst for adventure that took him to Hawaii and elsewhere in the South Seas. On Samoa he built a house on four hundred acres and lived there with his family until his death. To the natives of Samoa, he was known as Tusitala (Samoan for "Teller of Tales"). Though Stevenson was a man who traveled the globe, this poem reveals a true "family man" who is grateful for the love of his family "here assembled." It is a personal manifesto about life, a true thanks giving to the Lord.*

For the fruits of this creation,
    Thanks be to God.
For the gifts to every nation,
    Thanks be to God.
For the plowing, sowing, reaping,
Silent growth while we are sleeping,
Future needs in the earth's safe-keeping,
    Thanks be to God.

In the just reward of labor,
    God's will be done.
In the help we give our neighbor,
    God's will be done.
In the world-wide task of caring,
For the hungry and despairing,
In the harvest we are sharing,
    God's will be done.

— Fred Pratt Green (1903–2002)

Fred Pratt Green was a distinguished Methodist minister in England and is most noted for having written more than three hundred hymns and songs. His compositions were embraced by people across diverse theological, denominational, and national boundaries. During World War II, he was both a minister and air raid warden in an area along the Thames that saw a lot of warfare. In 1967, he supervised the creation of Hymns and Songs, *a supplement to* The Methodist Hymn Book. *He was honored when one of his hymns was included in the official service for the celebration of the jubilee of Queen Elizabeth II.*

Methodism is part of the Protestant tradition. The Protestant Reformation focused on three main matters of belief: the supreme authority of scripture, salvation by faith through faith in Christ, and the priesthood of all believers. In this, the Reverend Fred Pratt Green closely resembled John Wesley, the founder of Methodism, in the eighteenth century.

Radiant is the World Soul
Full of splendor and beauty
Full of life.
Of Souls Hidden,
Of treasures of the Holy Spirit,
Fountains of strength,
Of greatness and beauty.
Proudly I ascend
Toward the heights of the World Soul
That gives life to the universe.
How majestic the vision
Come, enjoy,
Come, find peace,
Embrace delight,
Taste and see that God is good.
Why spend your substance on what does not nourish
And your labor on what cannot satisfy?
Listen to me, and you will enjoy what is good,
And find delight in what is truly precious.

— Abraham Isaac Kook (1865–1935)

A mystic, philosopher, saint, and Talmudic scholar, Abraham Isaac Kook (Rav Kook) is considered the "father" of religious Zionism, an international political movement that was successful in establishing the State of Israel in 1948. In 1904, he came to Israel to assume a rabbinical post and responsibility for a new Zionist agricultural settlement at Jaffa. After World War I, he was appointed as first Chief Rabbi of Israel, though the state had not yet been born.

Rav Kook was a man of Halakha, a scholar of Jewish law encompassing rabbinic law, traditions, and nonreligious life. He maintained a remarkable openness to new ideas, such as the concept that modern Jewish nationalism, even at its most secular, expresses the divinity within the Jewish soul and signifies the beginning of the messianic age. He believed humankind has within itself a divine spark that motivates us to fulfill God's will even when we do not intend to do so. It is said that, like Mozart, he wrote spontaneously and never changed a word. He wrote about kodesh, *the inner "taste" of reality, which is the meaning of existence.*

All is beautiful,
All is beautiful,
All is beautiful, indeed.

Now the Mother Earth
and the Father Sky,
    Meeting, joining one another,
    Helpmates ever, they.
    All is beautiful,
    All is beautiful,
    All is beautiful, indeed . . .

And the white corn
And the yellow corn,
    Meeting, joining one another,
    Helpmates ever, they.
    All is beautiful,
    All is beautiful,
    All is beautiful, indeed . . .

Life-that-never-passeth,
Happiness-of-all-things,
    Meeting, joining one another,
    Helpmates ever, they.
    All is beautiful,
    All is beautiful,
    All is beautiful, indeed.

Now all is beautiful,
All is beautiful,
All is beautiful, indeed.

— Navaho Indian prayer

Navaho people sing this prayer, the Blessing of the Created World, as a benediction to all forms of life in the world, declaring them beautiful. Navajos use long song cycles to recount the elaborate mythology related to the ceremony that is called the Blessingway, which is composed of their rites and prayers concerned with healing, creation, harmony, and peace. The refrain "All is beautiful" indicates that this text is from a song — and it is a song magnificent on so many levels. It reveals reverence for earth, advises helping one another, and celebrates the beauty of corn and happiness. What more could one want to celebrate than the family, life, and togetherness?

I enter into the House of the Red Rock
Made holy by visiting gods,
And into the House of Blue Water
I am come.
Enter me, Spirit of my forgotten Grandmother,
That curtains of rain may hang
All dark before me,
That tall corn may shake itself
Above my head.

— Navajo and Blackfoot Indian prayer

This is a harvest seed prayer of the Navajo and Blackfoot Indians. The Blackfoot Indians were fierce warriors who, by the mid-nineteenth century, controlled a vast territory stretching from Saskatchewan to the southernmost waters of the Missouri. Later in that century, their population was decimated by the near extinction of the buffalo as well as by epidemics of smallpox and measles.

Blackfoots wore headdresses made of white eagle feathers with sharp, black tips that were highly regarded and symbolized acts of bravery. Their religious life centered on reverence for the Great Father. An adolescent warrior would undertake a vision quest in a remote area, where he would fast until he had a vision. He would be given a war song or dance by a guardian spirit and be told of the magical amulets — such as feathers, birds' beaks, or stones — that he should wear for power. The Blackfoot people celebrated the Sun Dance, which signified the renewal of both personal spirituality and the living earth. This was a time when kinships within both social and natural realms were reaffirmed, and, through this, prosperity and social harmony would be extended for another year.

Prayer 84

The sacred blue corn seed I am planting,
In one night it will grow and flourish,
In one night the corn increases,
In the garden of the House of God.

The sacred white corn seed I am planting
In one day it will grow and ripen
In one day the corn increases
In its beauty it increases.

— Navajo Indian prayer

This sacred Navajo food chant is intended to attract the attention of the gods so they will make the fields fertile and the crops grow — blue corn magically in one night, white corn in one day. The time frame is not realistic on earth, but "in the garden of the House of God" . . . all is possible. The prayer is addressed to two corn spirits: Blue Corn Woman and White Corn Maiden, spirit mothers of the Navajo people. Blue was the summer mother; White was the winter mother.

Corn originated in Mexico and was being cultivated by the Indians as far north as New England when the first European colonists arrived. The colonists' survival depended largely on corn. American Indians taught them to grow it, including some varieties of yellow corn that are still popular as food, as well as varieties with red, blue, pink, and black kernels, often banded, spotted, or striped, that today are regarded as ornamental and, in the United States, are called Indian corn. Corn is an important element in many religions and is a sacred food. To Navajos and other tribes, corn isn't just the grain that is eaten but is also a spiritual entity that gives people strength to survive.

He left it for us.

Something that should be for the people's happiness

They will be strong in body from it.

He left us all this food.

He scattered this all over the Earth.

Now we will give one thanks.

That he has left us all this food to live on.

On this Earth.

This is the way it should be in our minds.

— Seneca Indian thanks-giving prayer (circa 1800)

The Seneca were one of the most important tribes in the Iroquois League of Six Nations, composed of the Mohawk, Oneida, Cayuga, Onondaga, Tuscarora, and Seneca. The territory of the Seneca encompassed New York and Pennsylvania. They were lovers of eloquence, and their tribal culture fostered its cultivation. Oratory was an art among the Seneca Iroquois. They were the original occupants of the land, claiming to have lived here always and to have grown out of the soil like the trees of the forest. Their sustenance was based on the cultivation of corn, beans, and squash, which they called "the three sisters." Seneca women generally grew and harvested these crops, as well as gathered medicinal plants, roots, berries, nuts, and fruit. The Great Spirit "left us all this food to live on," they said; "now we will give one *thanks," expressing a profound sense of gratitude. The Seneca Nation of Indians today has a population of more than seventy-two hundred enrolled members.*

Prayer 86

I inform thee that I intend to eat thee.
Mayest thou always keep me to ascend,
So that I may always be able to reach
the tops of mountains,
and may I never be clumsy!
I ask this from thee, Sunflower-Root.
Thou are the greatest of all in mystery.

— Thompson River Indian prayer

The Thompson River Indians are an indigenous, or First Nations, people of Salish tribal ethnicity who inhabit the Thompson River area in British Columbia. The river is named after David Thompson, an English fur trader and mapmaker who in 1785 started working with Hudson's Bay Company.

The indigenous peoples of the Americas maintained agriculturally advanced societies for thousands of years, domesticating, breeding, and cultivating many plant species. The poetic beauty of the food prayer reveals the reverence that the people felt for a plant root — for life-sustaining food. The use of thee *and* thou *in this Indian food prayer was not customary to the Thompson River Indians but came from the English person who translated it. In British English,* thou *had fallen out of everyday use, even in familiar speech, sometime around 1650. The Book of Common Prayer, the foundational prayer book of the Church of England, first published in 1549 and revised in 1662, is replete with* thou's *and* thee's. "Mayest thou" *is very much of this era, and the English translation of this Salish Indian blessing is exquisite. Respect for and awe of food, in this case a root, is typical of Indian attitudes toward life-sustaining food from the Almighty.*

Prayer 87

Make us worthy, Lord,
To serve those people
Throughout the world who live and die
In poverty or hunger.

Give them, through our hands
This day their daily bread,
And by our understanding love,
Give peace and joy.

— Mother Teresa of Calcutta (1910–1997)

Prayer 88

Keep the joy of loving God in your heart and share this
joy with all you meet, especially your family. Be holy
— let us pray.

— Mother Teresa of Calcutta (1910–1997)

Mother Teresa of Calcutta, winner of the Nobel Peace Prize in 1979, dedicated her life to the service of the poorest of the poor all over the world. Born in 1910 in Macedonia, she was of Albanian descent. At the age of twelve, she strongly felt the call of God. She joined the Sisters of Loreto in 1928 and became a nun. At that time, she took the name Teresa after Saint Teresa of Lisieux, patroness of missionaries. From 1931 to 1948 she taught at Saint Mary's High School in Calcutta, but the suffering and poverty she saw outside the convent walls made such a deep impression on her that she got permission to leave the convent and work among the poor.

In 1950, Mother Teresa received permission from the Holy See to start her own order, the Missionaries of Charity, whose primary task was to love and care for destitute persons everywhere whom nobody else looked after. In 1965 the order became an International Religious Family by a decree of Pope Paul VI. Her society of missionaries has spread all over the world, including the former Soviet Union and eastern European countries. Mother Teresa was a living saint.

Prayer 89

Mother Earth, you who give us food,
whose children we are and on whom we depend,
please make this produce you give us flourish
and make our children and animals grow....

Children, the earth is the mother of man,
because she gives him food.

— Rigoberta Menchú (b. 1959)

*Rigoberta Menchú, winner of the Nobel Peace Prize in 1992, was born
into an Indian peasant family and raised in the Quiche branch of the
Mayan culture in Guatemala. She has become a voice of the poor and
oppressed indigenous peoples of her country. She engaged in social reform activities through the Catholic church and was active in the
women's rights movement while still a teenager. Such reform work
aroused considerable opposition in political circles, and the Menchú family was accused of taking part in guerrilla activities and was persecuted.
Menchú's father and brother were tortured and killed by the army. Her
mother died after having been arrested, tortured, and raped.*

*Menchú was determined to tell the world her story. She taught her-
self Spanish as well as Mayan languages other than her native Quiche.
In 1981, she went into hiding in Guatemala and then fled to Mexico.
In 1983, she told her life story to Elisabeth Burgos Debray. The result:
her famous autobiography* I, Rigoberta Menchú. *She kindly responded
to my request to provide an ancient food blessing from her culture.*

Prayer 90

When we eat the good bread,
we are eating months of sunlight,
weeks of rain and snow from the sky,
richness out of the earth.
We should be great, each of us radiant,
full of music and full of stories.
Able to run the way clouds do, able to
dance like the snow and the rain.
But nobody takes time to think that he eats all
these things and that sun, rain,
snow are all a part of himself.

— Monica Shannon (1905–1965)

During her brief writing career, Monica Shannon produced a variety of children's books and won the prestigious Newberry Medal.

Prayer 91

All that I have comes from my Mother!
I give myself over to this pot.
My thoughts are on the good,
the healing properties of this food.
My hands are balanced, I season well!

I give myself over to this pot.
Life is being given to me.
I commit to sharing, I feed others.
I feed She Who Feeds Me.

I give myself over to this gift.
I adorn this table with food.
I invite lovers and friends to come share.
I thank you for this gift.
All that I have comes from my Mother!

— Luisah Teish

The feminist movement's drive in the 1970s to re-vision our society at every level, including art, literature, and religious and spiritual practices, helped to popularize the Goddess religion. Many practices of the New Age movement and of New Age medicine are shamanistic in nature. Modern shamanism claims its methods will bring personal power, spiritual enlightenment, greater harmony with nature, psychological insight, and physical healing. One example of modern shamanism is Santeria, a syncretistic religion of Caribbean origin. It incorporates the worship of the Orisha (literally "head guardian") and beliefs of the Yoruba and Bantu people in southern Nigeria, Senegal, and the Guinea Coast. It also combines elements of worship from Roman Catholicism. Santeria's origins date back to the days of the slave trade, when Yoruba natives were forcibly transported from Africa to the Caribbean.

Luisah Teish is a writer and storyteller. She is a chief in the Ifa and Orisha tradition of southwestern Nigeria who is internationally known for her performances of African, Caribbean, and African American folklore and feminist myth. She is a priestess of Oshun, the Yoruba (West Africa) goddess of love, art, and sensuality.

Prayer 92

At candlelighting

May this Sabbath
lift our spirits,
lighten our hearts.

Sanctification over wine

Let us bless the source of life
that ripens fruit on the vine
as we hallow the Sabbath day
in remembrance of creation.

Washing the hands

Washing the hands, we call to mind
the holiness of the body.

Blessing over bread

Let us bless the source of life
that brings forth bread from the earth.

Blessing after the meal

Let us acknowledge the source of life
for the earth and for nourishment.
May we protect the earth
that it may sustain us,
and let us seek sustenance
for all who inhabit the world.

— Marcia Falk (b. 1946)

The philosophy of Marcia Falk, a politically liberal feminist-Jewish American poet, is accepted by both Reform and Reconstructionist Jews. Falk challenges the belief that Jews are a chosen people with a special covenant with God, since she rejects all distinctions made between men and women, homosexuals and heterosexuals, Jews and non-Jews. The idea of Israel as God's chosen people is a premise of rabbinic Judaism. She considers "chosenness" to be unethical, since it contradicts the notion that all humanity is created in the divine image and considers favoring one people over another as analogous to privileging one sex over another. The role of women in the synagogue is the most timely, but also potentially the most divisive, issue within all branches of Judaism. Historically, the role of Jewish women in public worship has been limited. Falk is expanding the Jewish horizon.

Prayer 93

We thank thee Lord
For happy hearts
For rain and sunny weather.
We thank thee Lord
For this food
And that we are together.

— Helen Armstrong Straub

He gives them shelter from life's stormy weather.
Gives them love to keep them together;
When life gets like a ship on a raging sea
And when the stage of life grows cold,
Somebody helps us play our role ...
If God is dead, who's that living in my soul?

If my soul had windows, I'd leave them open so the
  world could see
The ugly scars upon those hands that bled for you and
  me.
There's a bridge you can cross if you will
The toll was paid on Golgotha's hill.
If God is dead, who's that living in my soul?

— Lawrence Reynolds (1944–2000)

This country western song was written in 1969 and directed to Christians countering the belief that God was dead, a belief then gaining support in academia and that still thrives in many circles. Lawrence Reynolds and Harlan Howard collaborated on a number of hit country western songs. The American cowboy lifestyle portrayed in them is characterized by plain speaking and unvarnished truth. Anti-intellectuals often perceive themselves as champions of the "ordinary people," and this is the persuasive ethos of country western music.

Country western music originated as a blend of early mountain music, cowboy music, and music from the plantations of the Deep South.

Mmmm…*hmmm*, mymymy…and then I went on,
and God blessed me with my home, and I thank
him for that.…It may not be what you think it
should be…but I thank God that he gave it to me…
I got a roof over my head, thank you, Lord…I'm
not *braggin'*, children, just thankin' God.

— Marion Williams (1927–1994)

*Marion Williams was a legendary American gospel singer regarded as
one of the most powerful voices in American music history. She had an
astonishing four-octave range and influenced generations of gospel
singers. Williams was born into a family with a devout mother and mu-
sically inclined father. She sang with the Ward Singers, and with
them rose to fame. In 1991, she performed as a gospel singer in the film*
Fried Green Tomatoes, *which was dedicated to her. She was honored
as a MacArthur Fellow, an award that carries a prize also known as
the "genius grant." Her friend and music producer, Anthony Heilbut,
describes the hymn quoted in prayer 95 as a kind of "testifying" and
humble bragging that is associated with poor people.*

Prayer 96

Eternal Spirit of Justice and Love,
At this time of Thanksgiving we would be aware
   of our dependence on the earth and on the
   sustaining presence of other human beings
   both living and gone before us.
As we partake of bread and wine, may we
   remember that there are many for whom
   sufficient bread is a luxury, or for whom
   wine, when attainable, is only an escape.
Let our thanksgiving for Life's bounty include a
   commitment to changing the world, that
   those who are now hungry may be filled and
   those without hope may be given courage.
Amen.

— Prayer by the Congregation of Abraxas (1985)

This prayer, from the Book of Hours, originates with the Congregation of Abraxas, a Unitarian Universalist Order for Liturgical and Spiritual Renewal. Abraxas was an ancient Gnostic deity unifying contraries: good and evil, darkness and light, fragmentation and integration, fullness and void. Abraxas is the ambiguous nature of life. Abraxans do not choose between humanist and theist, the rational and the emotional, or the traditional and the experimental. Such opposites are inspired by religions of the East and traditions of the West, by preliterate ritual and secular science, and they inform worship today as practiced by all others.

Prayer 97

May the abundance of this table never fail
And never be less, thanks to the blessings of God,
Who has fed us and satisfied our needs.
To him be the glory for ever. Amen.

In peace let us eat this food
Which the Lord hath provided for us.
Blessed be the Lord in His gifts. Amen.

Glory be to the Father, and to the Son,
And to the Holy Ghost, now and always,
World without end. Amen.

— Armenian grace

The Armenian Church has been in existence since the days of the apostles, in the first century. The church was founded by two of Jesus' twelve apostles, Thaddeus and Bartholomew, who preached Christianity between AD 40 and AD 60. Armenia has been populated since prehistoric times, and religious scholars consider it to be the site of the biblical Garden of Eden, adjacent to Mount Ararat, where, the Bible relates, Noah's ark came to rest. Over the centuries, Armenia was conquered by Mongols, Turks, Persians, and Germans, and was part of the Soviet Union until establishing its independence in 1991.

Archbishop Mesrob Ashjian (1941–2003) faithfully served the Armenian Church for half a century. His legacy is the formation of an improved liturgical structure that unified the Armenian Apostolic Church. The above grace, taken from the Armenian Prelacy Diary, was provided to me by the archbishop.

Prayer 98

In a few moments of silence,
let each of us be mindful
of all we have for which to give thanks:
friends, food, hopes, health
and happy memories.

(a moment of silence observed)

So, in giving thanks,
we are blessed.
Amen.

— Traditional Christian blessing

This prayer, a blessing used in the Episcopal Church, employs a dramatic silent moment as a meaningful way to give thanks and reflect on life. The Episcopal Church in America is a branch of the worldwide Anglican Communion and derives from the Church of England. The latter established itself in North America at Jamestown, Virginia, in 1607. However, its clergy came to reject the supremacy of the British monarch, and, following the American Revolution, American Anglicans formed their own church. The Episcopal Church formally separated from the Church of England in 1789.

The Episcopal Church differs from the Roman Catholic Church in these principal ways: celibacy is not required of clergy, the church ordains women, and the diocese — not the church as a whole — is the primary unit of governance. The Episcopal Church's Book of Common Prayer revision dates from 1979 and is marked by linguistic modernization and an increased emphasis on the Eucharist as the principal service of the church.

Prayer 99

Help us, O God, to feed not only
upon bread that nourishes bone and sinew
but upon the radiance of night-blooming cereus,
and the purity of a selfless act, for we are a people
who must feed on bread, beauty, and compassion.

Bless our home, our Father,
that we cherish the bread before there be none,
discover each other for what we are . . .
while we have time.
Amen.

— Richard Wong

Richard Wong is a Christian minister who was born to Chinese immigrants in the Hawaiian Islands. His writing reflects Chinese and Hawaiian traditions. His prayers focus on island life and the beauty, concerns, and colors of the people there. In one prayer, for example, he asks, "Lord, please help me to be nice to 'strange-colored people.'"

Praised be God
Who gave me to eat and to drink.
I shall praise and bless God.

He helps the afflicted.
    Praise God.
He clothes the poor.
    Praise God.
He is bread for the hungry.
    Praise God.
He is a spring for the thirsty.
    Praise God.

He gives but none gives to Him.
    Praise God.
He lends but none lends to Him.
    Praise God.
He increases but none adds to Him.
    Praise God.
He teaches but none teaches Him.
    Praise God.

There is none save Him.
    Praise God.

— Liturgy of the Falasha of Abyssinia

Ethiopian Jews are better known the world over as Falashas, a native Jewish sect of Ethiopia, which is located in northeastern Africa. The Falasha are of Arabic origin and are known as Beta Israel, meaning "house of Israel." Beta Israel traditions claim that the Ethiopian Jews in general are descended from the lineage of Moses, some of whose children and relatives are said to have separated from the other children of Israel at the time of the Exodus and to have gone southward, down the Arabian coast along the Red Sea.

Falashas make up one of the oldest Jewish communities in the world; their history in Ethiopia is ancient and their origins are obscure. According to their own tradition, they are descended from Jews who accompanied Menelik, the son of King Solomon and the queen of Sheba, from Jerusalem to Ethiopia. For many years, Falashas thought they were the only remaining Jews. They continued to follow Judaism as it was practiced before the destruction of the temple in Jerusalem. Today, they number approximately twenty-five thousand — sixteen thousand of whom currently reside in Israel. The related Falash Mura are Ethiopian Jews who converted to Christianity. Many people believe that the Falasha people are the fabled lost tribe of Israel.

Most worshipful God,
you created humans to walk the earth with its
    abundance.
We beg of you, bless our family with riches and
    prosperity.
May our farms yield an abundant harvest,
our animals and chickens multiply.
And you our forefathers, we invite you to look after
    our well-being.
Ask and demand from us anything,
but protect us from all harm, illness, and evil spirits
which prowl the earth.
We will remember and honor you in the days to come.
We who partake of this abundant food rejoice
with those who rejoice and live long lives.
This is our heart's desire, and what our words express.
So let us feast.

— Prayer by the Kankana-ey tribe of the Igorot Indians

Igorot, *meaning "people of the mountains," is a name for the indigenous peoples of the Cordillera mountain region on the northern island of Luzon, in the Philippines. The Kankana-ey people built sloping terraces there to maximize farm space in the rugged mountain terrain. The famous Ifugao Banaue rice terraces are three thousand to six thousand years old, cover about four thousand square miles, and lie five thousand feet above sea level.*

The Portuguese explorer Ferdinand Magellan named the Philippines after King Philip II of Spain. In 1565 Magellan established the first Spanish settlements there, and, over the centuries, missionaries converted most of the inhabitants to Christianity. The Igorot religion is a belief in the spirit world of animism, which is widespread among primitive peoples. This pre-Christian native belief system has a hierarchy of spirits, the highest being the supreme deity, Lu-ma'-wig, the great spirit who dwells in the sky. All prayers for fruitage and increase — of people, of animals, and of crops — all prayers for deliverance from the fierce forces of the physical world, are made to him. The people pray: "A-li-ka' ab a-fi'-ik Ba-long'-long en-ta-ko' is a'-fong sang'-fu" (Come, soul of Ba-long'-long; come with us to the house to feast).

O Kané! Transform the earth
Let the earth move as in one piece
The land is cracked and fissured

The edible ferns yet grow, I Lono
Let kupukupu cover the dry lands
Gather potatoes as stones on the hills
The rain comes like the side of cliffs
The rain falling from Heaven
The potato falls from the heavens
The wild taro is only taro now
The taro of the mountain patches
The only food that is of the wilds
O Kané
O Kané and Lono! Gods of the husbandmen
Give life to the land

— Ancient Hawaiian harvest chant

This prayer thanks the gods for the harvest bounty and asks that the land be healed when it is ravaged by drought. Ancient Hawaiians gave ritualized thanks for the abundance of the earth and called upon the gods to provide rain and prosperity in the future. Lono, the god of fertility and rain, who was identified with southerly storms, could be seen in the black rain clouds on the Kona coast. Kané is the ruler of natural phenomena, such as the earth, stones, and fresh water. The edible ferns mentioned are kupukupu. Beyond food, this fern is also used for decorating the wrists and ankles of hula dancers.

So high we wave our hands to the rice lands,
To hail the grain blown to distant lands.
O come spirits of the rice field,
From where you've wandered.
Come back we plead.

— Igorot Indian prayer

This Igorot Indian harvest prayer comes from the highlands of northern Luzon. Customarily, a chicken is offered in thanks giving for a bountiful crop before being cooked for the family meal. Vegetal offerings are usually allowed to perish naturally, and prayer books used as offerings are set afire on special sacred stones or stone altars (batong buhay*).*

Igorot tribes believe that certain stars must come in line with the moon before important events like hunting expeditions, battles, and sacrifices may be undertaken. Among all the peoples of Indonesia, the mountain tribes of northern Luzon in the Philippines seem to stand alone in respect to cosmogonic myths, in that they lack almost entirely any myths about the origin of the universe. The world, according to their belief, has always existed, as has the upper world, or sky world.

Prayer 104

Salutations!

O Merciful God

Who provides food for the body and soul,

You have kindly granted what is spread before us.

We thank you.

Bless the loving hands that prepared this meal and us
who are to enjoy it, please.

Homage, homage,

Homage to thee!

— Tamil prayer

This prayer was composed in Tamil, the language of the people of southern India and Sri Lanka. The cultural identity, art, and religion of the Tamil people are among the oldest in the world: the recorded history of the Tamils goes back more than two thousand years. Tamil is one of the oldest of the many Dravidian languages. It is independent of Sanskrit, the classical language of Buddhism, Hinduism, and Jainism. Most Tamils are Hindus, but Islam and Christianity are represented among them as well.

Hinduism is a way of life more than a religion, and it focuses on the personal relationship between the devotee and the Supreme Being. A Hindu is one who accepts the authority of the Vedic scriptures and leads his or her life in accordance with dharma (righteousness). Sangam poetry is a body of Tamil classical literature created between the years 300 and 200 BC. Among the more than two thousand poems in this literature, many are set to music for stringed instruments and flute.

O God,
I am as one hungry for rice,
parched as one thirsty for tea.
Fill my so empty heart.
Amen.

— Chinese prayer

This lovely old poem from China makes an appeal for both physical and spiritual nourishment and expresses the longing to have one's heart filled with joy and redemption. Rice is a staple for a large part of the world's population, particularly in Asia. The earliest attested domestication of rice, a species of grass, took place in China around 7500 BC. Since humans have depended on rice for so long, it is understandable that it has been worshipped as a god and a gift and has been held in the highest esteem. The dominant religions in China are Buddhism and Taoism (or Daoism), which means "the Path" or "the Way."

O Supreme Lord, the giver of food,
Provide us with healthy and nourishing food.
Grant happiness to all those
That give food in charity.
May this food give us health and strength.

Offering this food is the Spirit of God.
This food is itself the Spirit of God.
It is offered in the Holy Name of God
For the sake of God.
Absorbed in this action for the sake of God,
May I attain the Supreme Godhead.

I dedicate this food
to the Supreme Godhead Sri Krishna.

— Gujarati mantra

This Hindu food prayer was composed in Gujarati, a language of India and neighboring Pakistan. A mantra is a religious or mystical poem whose words or vibrations instill mystical concentration in the devotee. Derived from Sanskrit, Gujarati is spoken by more than twenty-five million people. The majority of Gujarati-speaking Hindu are vegetarians who use clarified butter, or ghee, at meals. Ghee is also used in rituals. It is burned during marriages, funerals, and other ceremonies and sacrificed along with four other sacred substances: sugar, milk, yogurt, and honey. In the Mahabharata, ghee is mentioned as the root of sacrifice for one of the gods.

Prayer 107

Wisdom gives life to those who have it.
Happy is the body
that can nourish itself on food of the soul.

When you taste food,
if you know who it is that tastes it,
then you have known Him (Brahman).

— Sri Ramana Maharshi (1879–1950)

Sri Ramana was a mystic, a most holy Hindu man, distinguished by his silence and infrequent use of speech. Born in Tamil Nadu, in southern India, he led an ascetic life and relied on friends and devotees for his barest necessities. When he was sixteen, he had a premonition that he was going to die, and lay on the floor contemplating his death for a long time. His self-examination led him to realize that his body and his spirit were two different things, and he told himself: "I am not this perishable body. I and it [my body] are two different things. I am the indestructible I."

Sri Ramana's teachings about self-inquiry are considered a true path to knowledge. His self-inquiry, which takes the form of "Who am I," is considered one of the principal means to gain spiritual enlightenment. "Other than thoughts," he stated, "there is no such thing as the world." Followers of Sri Ramana have become teachers themselves, and they revere his humble way and spiritual insights. Around the world, several ashrams — hermitages in which sages live in tranquility amid nature — that propagate his teachings are named for him.

God of my needfulness,
grant me something to eat,
give me milk,
give me sons,
give me herds,
give me meat,
O my Father.

— African morning invocation

Indigenous African religions tend to revolve around animism and ancestor worship. A common thread in traditional African belief systems is the division of the spiritual world into "helpful" and "harmful" spirits. This prayer was provided by the Society for Promoting Christian Knowledge, the oldest Anglican mission organization (founded in 1698), which established missionaries in Africa to communicate the basic principles of the Christian faith. Ugandan evangelist Apolo Kivebulaya established the Anglican presence in Zaire in 1896. Christianity is the main religion in most of sub-Saharan Africa; in the northern part of the continent, the majority of the population is Muslim. Much of the Christian expansion in Africa today is the result of African evangelism.

Paleoanthropologists believe Africa is the earliest-inhabited land on earth and the place where human beings originated. The world's second-largest and second-most-populous continent, it contains fifty-three independent and sovereign countries, most of which still recognize borders drawn during the era of European colonialism. More than a thousand languages are spoken on this continent. Much of traditional African culture has become impoverished as a result of years of suppression and neglect by colonial and neocolonial regimes.

I shall sing a song of praise to God —
    Strike the chords upon the drum.

God who gives us all good things —
    Strike the chords upon the drum.

Wives, and wealth, and wisdom —
    Strike the chords upon the drum.

                        — Balubas praise song

The Balubas, a Bantu-speaking people of Zaire, were a cohesive tribe in the Congo during the seventeenth century. The Baluba creation story makes a connection between God's invisibility or unavailability and the endowment of humans with a soul or divine component longing for God. Bantu is a general term for more than four hundred different ethnic groups united by a common language and customs.

A majority of Africans consider themselves to be either Christian or Muslim. Missionary activity during the colonial period, together with modern evangelism practiced by American Pentecostal groups, established Christianity as the dominant religion on the continent. It is important to note that Christianity and Islam have been adapted in African contexts and incorporate elements of indigenous religions. They emphasize such things as healing and ancestor worship, which are relevant to African belief systems.

Prayer 110

God, we thank you for all your gifts.
This day, this night,
These fruits, these flowers,
These trees, these waters —
With all these treasures you have endowed us.
The heat of the sun, the light of the moon,
The songs of the birds and the coolness of the breeze,
The green, green grass like a mattress of velvet,
All owe their existence to your grace.
Dear God,
May we forever breathe the breath of your love
And every moment be aware
of your presence above.

— Pakistani prayer

This poem's devotional ardor reveals the beauty and flavor of the Punjabi language. Pakistan has an extensive history, one that is infused with the cultures of ancient India, Iran, and Afghanistan and reaches back to the Indus Valley civilization (2500–1500 BC). Incorporated into the British Raj in the nineteenth century, Pakistan did not become a modern state until 1947. Islam took root in Pakistan in AD 711. The central belief in Islam is that there is only one God, Allah, and that the Prophet Muhammad was his final messenger. Pakistani social life revolves around family and kin, and the household is the primary kinship unit. In its ideal form, it includes a married couple, their sons, their sons' wives and children, and unmarried offspring. The Sunni Muslim population of the Islamic Republic of Pakistan today makes up 80 percent of the whole.

Sweet is the work, my God, my King,
to praise thy name, give thanks and sing.

— Fasola hymn

*Puritan New England clergy, appalled at the poor quality of congre-
gational singing, instituted singing schools to teach people to sight sing.
The schools outgrew their purely church-centered focus and became an
integral part of the social life. In the rural areas of the Appalachians
and the Piedmont of the American South, the marriage of the New England singing-school music and the oral Celtic folk tune was completed,
and the folk hymn was born. Around 1800, these old-fashioned folk
hymns came to be written in "shape notes" — a right triangle for* fa,
an oval for sol, *a rectangle for* la, *and a diamond for* mi — *and over
time the music came to be known as fasola music, for the scale it com-
prised. From the southern Appalachians came folk hymns like "Amaz-
ing Grace" and "How Firm a Foundation" written in shape notes.*

Prayer 112

As thou hast set the moon in the sky
to be the poor man's lantern,
so let thy Light shine in my dark life
and lighten my path;
as the rice is sown in the water
and brings forth grain in great abundance,
so let thy word be sown in our midst
that the harvest may be great;
and as the banyan sends forth its branches
to take root in the soil,
so let thy Life take root in our lives.

— Hindu blessing

The banyan tree and rice place this blessing in the Indian Hindu context. The tree imagery of the poem resembles that of a lovely passage in the Bhagavad Gita describing a fig tree rooted in heaven with its branches streaming earthward — clearly a food-grace-God metaphor. An ancient Sanskrit verse speaks of the banyan this way: "Brahma-shaped at the root, Vishnu-shaped in the middle, and Shiva-shaped at the top, we salute you, the king of all trees."

The banyan is a tropical fig that bears continuously. Figs have higher quantities of fiber than any other dried or fresh fruit, so the fig really is a life-sustaining food source. The word banyan *is from Gujarati, the language spoken by more than forty million people in the Gujarat region of western India. No other Gujarati words have become established in English.*

Lord, you clothe the lilies,
you feed the birds of the sky,
you lead the lambs to pasture,
and the deer to the waterside,
you multiplied the loaves and fishes,
and changed the water to wine;
come to our table as giver,
and as our guest to dine.

— Presbyterian mealtime blessing

The Church of Scotland has no compulsory prayer book, although it does have a hymn book and its Book of Common Order. As do other Protestant denominations, the church recognizes two sacraments: baptism and Holy Communion (the Lord's Supper). Communion in the Church of Scotland today is open to Christians of all denominations, without precondition. Theologically, the Church of Scotland is Reformed (ultimately in the Calvinist tradition). However, its long-standing decision to respect "liberty of opinion on matters not affecting the substance of the faith" means it is relatively tolerant of a variety of theological positions.

Bless, O Lord, the plants,
the vegetation,
and the herbs of the field,
that they may grow
and increase to fullness
and bear much fruit.
And may the fruit of the land
remind us of the spiritual fruit
we should bear.

— Coptic Orthodox liturgy

The Church of Egypt is the Coptic Orthodox Church of Alexandria, which, according to tradition, the apostle Mark established in AD 42. Mark was the first patriarch of Alexandria, who exercised authority in matters of the early church. Christianity practiced in the Eastern Orthodox Church is the oldest form of Christianity in Africa and one of the earliest forms of Christianity in the world. Its adherents claim it is the original, unchanged, and historical church established by Jesus and the apostles.

The word orthodox *means "correct worship" and is the term the church adopted during the great schism between East and West to distinguish Eastern Orthodoxy from the (Western) Roman Catholics. The primary causes of the schism were disputes over papal authority — the pope claimed he held authority over the Eastern Greek-speaking churches.* Coptic *in general refers to the Christian natives of Egypt. The Coptic language is a direct descendant of the ancient Egyptian language once written in hieroglyphics.*

We entreat thee, O Lord,
mercifully to bless the air and the dews,
the rains and the winds;
that through thy heavenly benediction all may
be saved from dearth and famine,
and enjoy the fruits of the earth in abundance
and plenty;
for the eyes of all wait upon thee, O Lord,
who givest them their meat in due season.

— Indian prayer

This celebratory prayer is used in the Eucharist by the Church of India. It employs imagery especially meaningful to Indian cultures, with its benediction that all may be "saved from dearth and famine." The British presence in India dates back to the early part of the seventeenth century. In 1600, Elizabeth I, monarch of the United Kingdom, acceded to the demand by many merchants that a royal charter be given to a new trading company, which came to be called the "Governor and Company of Merchants of London, Trading into the East-Indies." Commerce then paved the way for Anglican missionaries.

India had been the object of evangelicals' ambitions since the British East India Company's charter was granted. In 1698 the Society for Promoting Christian Knowledge was founded. The Anglican Church in India was named the "Church of India in communion with the Church of England." The church had to hold fast to the fundamentals as laid down in the Lambeth Conference, whose doctrine was articulated in the Book of Common Prayer. But there were accommodations for the cultural needs of the Indian peoples.

Prayer 116

O God, you have formed heaven and earth;
You have given me all the goods
    that the earth bears!

Here is your part, my God.
Take it!

— Pygmy prayer

The indigenous peoples of the Congo Basin in central West Africa are forest-centered hunter-gathers known as Pygmies. A hunter-gatherer society is one whose primary diet depends on the direct procurement of edible plants and animals from the wild. Hunting and gathering was the only subsistence strategy employed by human societies for more than two million years, until the end of the Paleolithic era. Given the scarcity of food among hunter-gatherers, the notion of sharing as thankfulness is extraordinary.

Earth, when I am about to die
I lean upon you.
Earth, while I am alive
I depend upon you.

— Ashanti prayer

The Ashantis of Central Ghana say this prayer to the rhythm of "talking drums" every three weeks at a ceremony honoring their ancestors. The Ashanti recognize a universal God, Onyame, but they do not exclude gods associated with other spirits by whom a priest may be possessed. This makes it possible for, say, a traditional priest to also be a Roman Catholic. Traditional religion does not require regular attendance. The gods and the spirits of the ancestors are always present.

In Ashanti culture, a man wishing to consult the fetish priest or the chief addresses his remarks to an individual known as the Linguist, who then passes them on and returns the reply, even though all three people are present together. The Linguist is an intermediary who acts as a buffer to reduce the severity of utterances and so save delicate situations. Western society has no corresponding role. The Ashanti speak various dialects of Twi, a language rich in proverbs. Euphemisms are common, especially concerning events connected with death. Rather than say "The king has died," for example, one would say "A mighty tree has fallen."

Enter, O Lord, enter this home and bless each of us one by one and also bless our loved ones. Grant that we enjoy the fruits of your redemptive peace.

With a blessed glance deliver us from anything that might harm us. Shower your divine grace over each of us that we might share this bread without sorrow. With your power, Lord, free us from anything that might hurt us in mind, soul, and body. Amen.

— Sister Judith Marie Saenz

While a very young girl, Sister Judith Marie Saenz learned this blessing prayer from her aunt in Laredo, Texas. Sister Saenz grew up in a faith-filled family. "We were poor but I did not realize we were poor," she has said. Prayer and worship were important in their family, and they always worshipped together and prayed before meals. This blessing prayer, a prime example of oral tradition, was originally in Spanish, and Sister Saenz has translated it.

Prayer 119

All life is your own,
All fruits of the earth
Are fruits of your womb,
Your union, your dance.
Lady and Lord,
We thank you for blessings and abundance.
Join with us, Feast with us, Enjoy with us!
Blessed be.

— Starhawk (b. 1951)

Starhawk is the author of many works celebrating the Goddess move-
ment and Earth-based, feminist spirituality. She is a pagan and a witch.
She has played a pivotal role in bringing Goddess worship to the reli-
gious forefront, where one can turn to the Goddess to deepen one's sense
of personal pride, develop inner power, and integrate mind, body, and
spirit. Starhawk's mind and energy have been an agent for the modern-
day reemergence of Wicca as a Goddess-worshipping religion. She has
left her mark on the feminist spiritual consciousness, with its broad
philosophy of harmony with nature, of human concord, sexual libera-
tion, creativity, and healthy pleasure, as expressed and celebrated in
a freewheeling worship of the universe.

We return thanks to our mother,
    the earth, which sustains us.
We return thanks to the rivers and streams,
    which supply us with water.
We return thanks to all herbs,
    which furnish medicines for the cure of our diseases.
We return thanks to the corn, and to her sisters,
    the beans and squashes,
    which give us life.
We return thanks to the bushes and trees,
    which provide us with fruit.
We return thanks to the wind,
    which, moving in the air, has banished diseases.
We return thanks to the moon and stars,
    which have given to us their light
    when the sun was gone.
We return thanks to our grandfather Hé-no,
    that he has protected his grandchildren
    from witches and reptiles,
    and has given to us his rain.
We return thanks to the sun,
    that he has looked upon the earth
    with a beneficent eye.
Lastly, we return thanks to the Great Spirit,
    in whom is embodied all goodness,
    and who directs all things
    for the good of his children.

— Iroquois Indian prayer

Prayer 121

O Great Spirit,
Creator and source of every blessing,
we pray that you will bring peace to all
our brothers and sisters of this world.

Give us wisdom to teach our children to love,
to respect and to be kind to each other.
Help us to learn to share all the good things that you
provide for us.

Bless all who share this meal with us today.

We ask your special blessing on those who are
hungry today, especially little children.

Help us to be just and to bring your peace to all the
earth.

Praise and Thanksgiving be to you, Amen.

— Author unknown

Whenever the Confederate Lords shall assemble for
the purpose of holding a council, the Onondaga Lords
shall open it by expressing their gratitude to their
cousin Lords and greeting them, and they shall make
an address and offer thanks to the earth where men
dwell, to the streams of water, the pools, the springs
and the lakes, to the maize and the fruits, to the
medicinal herbs and trees, to the forest trees for their
usefulness, to the animals that serve as food and give
their pelts for clothing, to the great winds and the
lesser winds, to the Thunderers, to the Sun, the mighty
warrior, to the moon, to the messengers of the Creator
who reveal his wishes and to the Great Creator who
dwells in the heavens above, who gives all the things
useful to men, and who is the source and the ruler of
health and life. Then shall the Onondaga Lords
declare the council open. The council shall not sit
after darkness has set in.

— Iroquois Confederacy constitution

This is the Great Binding Law that served as the constitution of the Iroquois Confederacy, an organization that formed about 1575. The confederacy was made up of six nations: the Onondaga, the Oneida, Seneca, Mohawk, Cayuga, and the Tuscarora. The Iroquois core beliefs included the conception of life as a struggle between the forces of good and evil, and the conception of the "All-Father," an all-embracing deity. They believed that spirits animated all of nature and controlled the changing of the seasons. Key festivals coincided with the major events of the agricultural or hunting calendar, and food was the center of Iroquois culture, for sustenance and ceremony. The name Iroquois *comes from the phonetic sound of their phrase* hiro kone, *which they uttered when finished speaking.* Hiro kone *translates as "I have spoken," meaning "I have spoken in truth." The honor and integrity of the tribe is well articulated in the above philosophy, which is an eloquent thanks giving.*

Deep peace
    of the running wave to you,
Deep peace
    of the quiet earth to you,
Deep peace
    of the flowing air to you,
Deep peace
    of the shining star to you.

— Gaelic blessing

Gaelic *used as an adjective means "pertaining to the Gaels," a collective term that describes people from Ireland, Scotland, and the Isle of Man. Gaelic language and culture have existed since Roman times. This blessing comes from an unknown source; however, it has nuances that evoke the spirit of Saint Patrick, the fifth-century missionary who, during the seventh century, became the patron saint of Ireland and served as the foundation for Irish Christianity. Patrick was born in Roman Britain, and when he was sixteen he was captured by Irish raiders and carried off to be a slave in Ireland, where he remained for years. He prayed daily and one day heard a voice saying his "ship was ready." Patrick escaped on foot and went to a port hundreds of miles away.*

The nautical imagery of the running waves, the flowing air, and the shining (navigational) star are together a metaphor for escape from treachery to peace and salvation. Legend credits Patrick with teaching the Irish about the concept of the Trinity by showing them the shamrock, a three-leaf clover, using it to portray the Christian dogma of "three divine persons in the one God."

These offers are not piled high.
They are not heaped high.
It is only a small bit,
It is only a humble amount.
But grant me your divine pardon.
Grant us your divine forgiveness.
Receive this humble branch of pine,
Receive this humble bit of incense,
Receive this humble cloud of smoke.
Receive then; your holy sun has gone over the hill,
Your holy ear has passed.
Take this for the holy end of the year,
Take this for the holy end of the day.

— Zinacanteán Indian prayer

This Indian prayer is most humble and confesses that the offerings to God are inadequate. It was translated by Father Joseph Asturias who served in the Dominican Mission for twenty-one years until his death in 1995. The Dominican Mission Foundation continues to support the Dominican friars and sisters in Mexico, especially Ocosingo, Altamirano, and Chiapas, ministering to 200,000 Indians in various ethnic groups living in 1,000 communities.

Prayer 125

For the hay and the corn
    and the wheat that is reaped,
For the labor well done,
    and the barns that are heaped,
For the sun and the dew
    and the sweet honeycomb,
For the rose and the song,
    and the harvest brought home —
Thanksgiving! Thanksgiving!

                        — English traditional hymn

This prayer is a traditional celebration of the harvest. In Britain, thanks have been given for successful harvests since pagan times, and people have celebrated by singing, praying, and decorating churches with baskets of fruit and food — these were harvest festivals. Harvest comes from an Anglo-Saxon word haerfest, *which means "autumn." It refers to the season for reaping and gathering grain and other farm and garden produce. The full moon nearest the autumnal equinox is called the harvest moon, and in ancient times harvest festivals were traditionally held on the Sunday nearest the harvest moon.*

Early settlers took the idea of harvest thanks giving to North America, and pilgrims celebrated Thanksgiving there in 1621. The British tradition of holding harvest festivals in churches began in 1843, and these included singing thanks-giving hymns such as "Come, Ye Thankful People, Come" and "All Things Bright and Beautiful."

Footprints I make! I go to the field with eager haste.

Footprints I make! Amid rustling leaves I stand.

Footprints I make! Amid yellow blossoms I stand.

Footprints I make! I stand with exultant pride.

Footprints I make! I hasten homeward with a burden of
gladness.

Footprints I make! There's joy and gladness in my
home.

Footprints I make! I stand amidst a day of
contentment.

— Osage Indian prayer

*This Osage song celebrates the first corn of the season. It is sung by a
mother as she runs to tell her children the exciting news of their new crop.
This harvest song has been passed down through oral tradition over
many generations. Before the arrival of Europeans, the Osage Indians
lived along the Osage and Missouri rivers in what is now western
Missouri. French explorers first heard of them in 1673. The seasonal
movements of the Osage, a seminomadic people with a lifestyle based
on hunting, foraging, and gardening, brought them annually into
northwestern Arkansas. The men hunted bison, deer, elk, and bear, and
the women butchered the animals and dried or smoked the meat and prepared the hides. The women also gathered wild plant foods and, at the
summer villages, tended gardens of corn, beans, squash, and pumpkins.*

Prayer 127

I am sorry I had to kill thee, Little Brother,
But I had need of thy meat.

My children were hungry and crying for food.
Forgive me, Little Brother.

I will do honor to thy courage, thy strength,
    and thy beauty.

See, I will hang thine horns on this tree.
I will decorate them with red streamers.

Each time I pass, I will remember thee and
    do honor to thy spirit.

I am sorry I had to kill thee.
Forgive me, Little Brother.

See, I smoke to thy memory,
I burn tobacco.

— Plains Indian prayer

In this prayer an Indian addresses the deer he has killed. Out of respect for the life taken, he begs its forgiveness and expresses pity. Religious traditions of aboriginal peoples around the world tend to be heavily influenced by their methods of acquiring food, whether by hunting wild animals or by agriculture. Native American spirituality is no exception. Native American rituals and beliefs show a blending of interest in promoting and preserving their hunting and horticulture.

Their religious beliefs are grounded in the idea that a soul, or spirit, exists in all people and animals. Individuals, families, and the tribe must observe a complex system of taboos to assure that animals will continue to make themselves available to the hunters. Many rituals and ceremonies are performed before and after hunting expeditions to assure hunting success.

The beauty of the trees,
the softness of the air,
the fragrance of the grass,
    speaks to me.

The summit of the mountain,
the thunder of the sky,
the rhythm of the sea,
    speaks to me.

The strength of the fire,
the taste of salmon,
the trail of the sun,
and the life that never goes away,
    they speak to me.

And my heart soars.

— Chief Dan George (1899–1981)

Chief Dan George was a gifted actor, writer, and chief of the Salish Band in Burrard Inlet, British Columbia. He first came to prominence in a supporting role as the Indian who adopts the character played by Dustin Hoffman in Arthur Penn's film Little Big Man *(1970), for which he received an Academy Award nomination. The above poem is from his book* My Spirit Soars. *He tried to use his writing and media roles to give an accurate depiction of American Indian beliefs and values. He wrote several books and gave numerous speeches on behalf of his people. His words are moving and reach deep into the hearts of all people as he pours out his sadness for the plight of Indian people everywhere.*

This food comes from the Earth and the Sky,
It is the gift of the entire universe
and the fruit of much hard work;
I vow to live a life which is worthy to receive it.

— Grace of the Bodhisattva Buddhists

Buddhism offers us a radical approach to life, and its teachings are both challenging and inspiring. Buddha gave clear, direct, and comprehensive instruction on how to transform all aspects of one's life in the light of the dharma, the underlying order in nature, with an emphasis on human nature being in accord with that order.

Buddhist centers worldwide offer meditation classes, courses, retreats, study programs, and other Buddhist practices. Reading some of the oldest Buddhist texts today may lead one to find ways to apply them in daily life. Buddhist retreats and chanted meditations are intended to make the mind calm and peaceful. If your mind is peaceful, it will be free from worries and mental discomfort, and you can experience true happiness; but if your mind is not peaceful, you will find it difficult to be happy. The chanted meditations, known as pujas, *follow a range of Buddhist prayers. Buddha told his followers, "Where the Noble Eight-fold Path is found, there those endowed with wisdom are found."*

The garden is rich with diversity
With plants of a hundred families
In the space between the trees
With all the colors and fragrances
Basil, mint, and lavender,
God keep my remembrance pure,
Raspberry, Apple, Rose,
God fill my heart with love,
Dill, anise, tansy,
Holy winds blow in me.
Rhododendron, zinnia,
May my prayer be beautiful
May my remembrance O God
    be an incense to thee
In the sacred grove of eternity
As I smell and remember
The ancient forest of earth.

— Chinook Psalter (1891–1904)

Chinook Indians are Native Americans of the Pacific Northwest who live along the Columbia River in Oregon and Washington. Meriwether Lewis and William Clark encountered the Chinook on their expedition in 1805. The Chinook were a hedonistic society with a penchant for entertaining and celebrating life. They had vivid aesthetics and an enhanced appreciation for colors, fragrances, and herbs, which is evident from this blessing. Missionaries in their efforts to convert the Native Americans went as far as to translate hymns and Bible texts into Chinook.

A Catholic missionary, Father Jean-Marie Le Jeune taught at Indian missions in the region. Beginning in 1891 he edited and published a pamphlet devoted to instructing local Indians in the Christian faith. This pamphlet, undated, contains music and words for worship. The "Chinook Psalter" most likely did not exist as a single published text. Father Le Jeune developed stenographic symbols for Chinook jargon and used those symbols in a religious newspaper of thirteen volumes, published from 1891 to 1904.

A psalter is a song, or a variation on a verse, usually taken from the book of Psalms and most often used in a church service as part of the liturgy. The Chinook language was in common use until the 1920s and is still being spoken today, largely as a result of efforts by a preservationist community centered on several tribal groups in the Northwest.

First, let us reflect on our own work
    and the effort of those who brought us this food.
Secondly, let us be aware of the quality of our deeds
    as we receive this meal.
Thirdly, what is most essential
    is the practice of mindfulness
    which helps us transcend greed, anger, and
    delusion.
Fourthly, we appreciate this food
    which sustains the good health of our body and
    mind.
Fifthly, in order to continue our practice for all beings
    we accept this offering.

— Zen Buddhist prayer

Known as the Five Reflections, this prayer is a traditional Rinzai Zen text. Rinzai Zen was brought to Japan in 1191. Because the Zen tradition emphasizes direct communication over scriptural study, the role of the Zen teacher has traditionally been central. The essence of the philosophy lies in the koan (literally, "public case") — a story or dialogue generally related to Zen or other Buddhist history. A koan is a question or statement of Zen Buddhism designed to probe intelligence and understanding. One famous koan is "Two hands clap and there is a sound; what is the sound of one hand?" The response to the koan involves a transformation of perspective or consciousness. The Zen student's mastery of a given koan is presented to the teacher in a private interview.

According to one view, a koan embodies a realized principle or law of reality. Movements in fine art tend to have much in common thematically with the study of koans and realizations. D. T. Suzuki, author of books and essays on Zen Buddhism, was instrumental in spreading interest in Zen satori (awakening) worldwide.

Prayer 132

For the order and constancy of nature;
For the beauty and bounty of the world;
For day and night, summer and winter, seed-time and
　　harvest;
For the varied gifts of loveliness and use which every
　　season brings:

We praise thee.

— John Hunter (1848–1917)

Prayer 133

Greeting, Father's Clansman,
I have just made a robe for you, this is it.
Give me a good way of living.
May I and my people safely reach the next year.
May my children increase; when my sons go to war,
may they bring horses.
When my son goes to war, may he return with black
    face.
When I move, may the wind come to my face,
may the buffalo gather toward me.

This summer may the plants thrive,
may the cherries be plentiful.
May the winter be good, may illness not reach me.
May I see the new grass of summer,
may I see the full-sized leaves when they come.
May I see the spring.
May I with all my people safely reach it.

— Crow Indian prayer

This prayer is a thanks offering and a plea for a good life. The Crow Indians are a Native American people living in Montana. Crow is a kinship system used to define family. The Crow are matrilineal, and women play a highly significant role within the tribe. This prayer is an eloquent petition to the Father's Clansman asking for increasing family, for abundant food, and for a good life where the "buffalo gather toward me." The Crow were a nomadic people, and food was never assured. They perfected the buffalo jump, a technique for herding bison and driving them over a cliff. After the advent of the continental railroad, the drive west by settlers, and the near extinction of the buffalo, life was arduous.

Prayer 134

So often bread is taken for granted,
Yet there is so much of beauty in bread —
Beauty of the sun and the soil,
Beauty of human toil.
Winds and rains have caressed it,
Christ, Himself, blessed it.

— Christian prayer

Pity me, pity me!
Father, pity me!

Pity me, pity me!
Father, pity me!

I cry for thirst:
    see, I am crying!
I cry for thirst:
    see, I am crying!

I have naught to eat,
I've nothing;
I have naught to eat,
I've nothing.

— Arapaho Indian chant

This is an abject plea for food and sustenance. The Arapaho Indians lived in Minnesota and North Dakota. They lived in teepees, which the women made from buffalo skins. They were nomadic traders and were subject to the vicissitudes of the seasons, weather, and the ill fortune that accompanied the settlers' expansion into the West. Ever starving, they were referred to as "dog eaters" (for the obvious reason) by other Native Americans. The Arapaho performed a Sun Dance in the summer when the Arapaho bands came together for a ceremony intended to guide warriors. These warriors would receive a vision in which they were given a guardian spirit. The Arapaho still execute the Sun Dance, using their own distinctive rituals and methods of performance.

O thou cereal deity, we worship thee.
Thou hast grown very well this year,
and thy flavor will be sweet.
Thou art good.
The goddess of fire will be glad, and
we also shall rejoice greatly.
O thou god, O thou divine cereal,
do thou nourish the people.
I now partake of thee.
I worship thee and give thee thanks.

— Ainu prayer

The Ainu are traditionally animists who live mainly on the Japanese archipelago, and the prayer is an homage to the god millet: "O thou divine cereal . . . I worship thee and give thee thanks." Millet is a cereal crop grown in Asia since the sixth century BC. The cultivation of millet was once more prevalent than that of rice.

Animism is a belief in spirits — that is, mystical, supernatural, or imagined entities, beings, gods, or souls that inhabit nature and ordinary things such as animals, foods, and objects. Animistic belief was the most primitive and essential form of religion. The idea of the soul is the nucleus of the animistic system: spirits are only souls that have made themselves independent, and the souls of animals, plants, and objects were created analogous to humans.

The lands around my dwelling
Are more beautiful
From the day
When it is given me to see
Faces I have never seen before.
All is more beautiful,
All is more beautiful,
And life is thankfulness.
These guests of mine
Make my house grand.

— Eskimo prayer

The Eskimo inhabit the arctic region of northern Canada and Alaska. This prayer is expressly for a life that is bursting with "thankfulness." Whereas we might see bleakness in the frozen tundra, this prayer signals praise for the beauty of the land and for guests who make the home "grand." Guests are considered a blessing.

In Alaska and northern Canada, the Eskimo are known as the Inuit. The Intuit live in large paternal kinship groups. They practice many mystical and animistic rituals relating to the hunting of arctic marine animals, which are the foundation on which most Eskimo cultures rest. Eskimo kissing is named for the gesture of rubbing noses, a nonromantic greeting between two people that is equivalent to our shaking hands.

Prayer 138

Nicely, nicely, nicely, away in the East,
the rain clouds care for little corn plants
as a mother cares for her baby.

— Zuni Indian corn ceremony

This brief prayer chant is full of the imagery of love and thankfulness, with the rain caring for the corn, and the mother caring for her baby. Zuni are deeply religious, and they believe that everything shares a common spirit, that everything is interconnected. They also believe that gods reside in the lakes of Arizona and New Mexico. During religious festivals, chiefs and shamans carry out two different types of ceremonies. Song and dance accompany masked performances by the chiefs, and the shamans pray to the gods for favors ranging from fertile soil to abundant amounts of rain. The shamans play an important role in the community, as they are looked to for guidance, general knowledge, and healing. The Zuni people are a somewhat mysterious tribe. But though they are reclusive and isolated, they are well known for their beautiful silver jewelry and sculpture.

Prayer 139

O God, our Father,
be Thou the Unseen guest at our table,
and fill our Hearts with Thy Love.

— Author unknown

163

Rev'rent our hearts turn unto the
One who brings to us
Long life and children, peace,
And the gifts of strength and food.
Rev'rent our hearts turn unto our Mother Corn!

Rev'rent our hearts turn unto the
Source whence comes to us
Long life and children, peace,
and the gifts of strength and food,
Gifts from Tira'wa, sent through our Mother Corn.

— Pawnee Indian prayer

This prayer is from the Hako ceremony, and it asks for more children so that the tribe may increase and be strong. It also asks that the people may have long life, enjoy plenty, and be happy and at peace. "Rev'rent our hearts" is complete thankfulness. The dominant power in Pawnee experience was Tira'wa, generally spoken of as "Father." Mother Corn was a woman who succored a hungry tribe, frequently taking in an orphan as a foster child. Her gift was the all-nourishing sacred food. Pawnee religious ceremonies were connected with the cosmic forces and the heavenly bodies. A series of ceremonies relative to the bringing of life began with the first thunder in the spring and culminated at the summer solstice, but the series did not close until the maize, called "mother corn," was harvested.

Prayer 141

Thank God for home,
and crisp, fair weather,
and loving hearts
That meet together —
And red, ripe fruit
And golden grain —
And dear Thanksgiving
    Come again!

— Nancy Byrd Turner (1880–1971)

I'm an Indian.
I think about common things like this pot.
The bubbling water comes from the rain cloud.
It represents the sky.
The fire comes from the sun
which warms us all, men, animals, trees.
The meat stands for the four-legged creatures,
our animal brothers,
who gave of themselves so that we should live.
The steam is living breath.
It was water, now it goes up to the sky,
becomes a cloud again.
These things are sacred.
Looking at that pot full of good soup,
I am thinking how, in this simple manner,
The great Spirit takes care of me.

— John Lame Deer (1903–1976)

John Lame Deer was a Sioux Indian who, as a young man, lived a rough and wild life. One day he visited a house that held the original peace pipe given to the Sioux by White Buffalo Woman, a sacred woman of supernatural origin who also gave the Lakota — one of a group of seven tribes that made up the Great Sioux Nation — their Seven Sacred Rituals. The keeper of the pipe told Lame Deer she had been waiting for him for some time. This transformed him from a hoodlum to a holy man. "With this holy pipe," she said, "you will walk like a living prayer. With your feet resting upon the earth and the pipestem reaching into the sky, your body forms a living bridge between the Sacred Beneath and the Sacred Above. Wakan Tanka smiles upon us, because now we are as one: earth, sky, all living things, the two-legged, the four-legged, the winged ones, the trees, the grasses. Together with the people, related, one family. The pipe holds them all together."

She was right. In the 1970s he became well known to the American public at a time when indigenous culture and spirituality were going through a period of rebirth through the efforts of the American Indian Movement, an activist organization that came to national prominence. Lame Deer was greatly admired. A full-blooded Sioux, he was many things in the white man's world — rodeo clown, painter, prisoner. But above all he was a holy man of the Lakota tribe.

Prayer 143

Thank you, heavenly Father,
for my bread,
my dad and mother and my bed. Amen.

— Child's prayer of thanks

We eat and we are revived, and we give thanks
to the lives that were ended to nourish our own.
May we merit their sacrifice, and honor
their sparks of holiness
through our deeds of loving kindness.

We give thanks to the Power that makes for a Meeting,
for our table has been a place of dialogue and friendship.

We give thanks to Life.
May we never lose touch with the simple joy and wonder
of sharing a meal.

— Rabbi Rami M. Shapiro (b. 1951)

The wonderful world according to Rabbi Rami M. Shapiro:

Gemilut chasadim: *Seek out opportunities for doing acts of loving
kindness daily.*

Shmirat halashon: *Use your thoughts and words to heal rather than
harm.*

Shalom bayit: *Continually improve your ability to love, befriend,
and parent.*

Kavod av v'em: *Honor your parents and elders by seeing to their
welfare and listening to their wisdom.*

Mezuzah: *Place mezuzot on the doorposts of your homes as reminders
to align yourself with godliness.*

Prayer 145

Bless us, O Lord, and these Thy gifts which we
    are about to receive
From Thy bounty, through Christ our Lord.
Amen.

In Latin:

Benedic, Domine, nos et haec tua dona quae de
    tua largitate sumus sumpturi. Per Christum
    Dominum nostrum.
Amen.

— Traditional Catholic prayer before meals

Prayer 146

Give us this day our daily bread.

— Matthew 6:11, Bible, American Standard Version

Prayer 147

Go, eat your bread with joy,
and drink your wine with a merry heart.

— Ecclesiastes 9:7, Bible, New King James Version

Prayer 148

Bless our hearts
to hear in the
breaking of bread
the song of the universe.

— Father John Giuliani (b. 1932)

This prayer was composed by Father John Giuliani, a priest of the Diocese of Bridgeport, Connecticut, and spiritual director of the Benedictine Grange in Redding, Connecticut. He was one of thirty-three international artists, writers, and social justice advocates who in 2006 won a Mother Teresa Award, given to those who have beatified the world through arts, social justice, and spiritual contributions. The award is conferred on individuals who create beauty by celebrating the spirit. Painter, writer, and spiritual leader, Father John Giuliani founded inner-city soup kitchens that have become sanctuaries for the poor and homeless in Bridgeport and Norwalk, Connecticut.

The Benedictine Grange was established in 1977 when Father John Giuliani received permission from Bishop Curtis of Bridgeport to found a small monastic community in Redding. Each Sunday, the liturgy is celebrated in a pre–Civil War barn.

Prayer 149

God be in my bread
God be in my head
God be in my body
God be in my arms
God be in me
God be all around me

God be in all things
God be.

— William C. Segal (1904–2000)

The philosopher and painter William C. Segal began his career as a journalist. In the 1940s he met P. D. Ouspensky and G. I. Gurdjieff. After World War II, through his friendship with Daisetz Suzuki, he was able to spend considerable periods of time at the main Rinzai and Soto monasteries in Japan. He is the author of many philosophical essays and books.

Prayer 150

A table is not blessed if it has fed no scholars.

— Yiddish proverb

A Grace in American Sign Language

Bless   *us*   *(O) Lord*   *and*

thy   *gifts*   *which*

we   *are about to*   *receive*

from   *thy*   *bounty*   *Amen*

A Child's Grace in American Sign Language

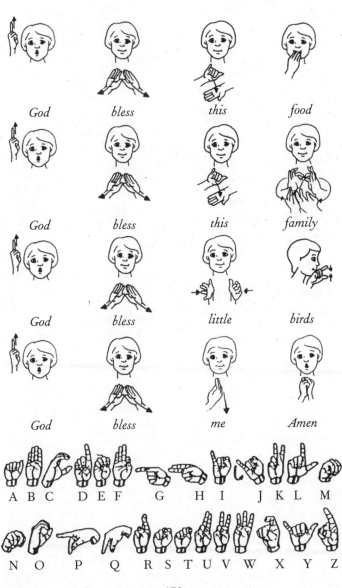

God   bless   *this*   *food*

God   bless   *this*   *family*

God   bless   *little*   *birds*

God   bless   *me*   *Amen*

A B C   D E F   G   H I   J K L M

N O   P   Q   R S T U V W X Y Z

"Bless This Food" in Nineteen Languages

Bless this food
English

Benedicite hunc cibum
Latin

Bendita sea esta comida
Spanish

Benis ce repas
French

Benedetto questo cibo
Italian

Segne diese speisen
German

Ευλογειτε Εκεινον Αρτον
Eulogayte Ekaynon Arton
Classical Greek

بارك هذا الطعام
Barek natra aet'taam
Arabic

БЛАГОСЛОВИ ЭТУ ЕДУ!
Blagaslavee aetoo yedoo
Russian

בָּרְכוּ אֶת הָאוֹכֶל
Bareku et he'okel
Hebrew

टे स्वानेको आशिर्याटें दो
Ae kanae koo asheez doo
Hindi

Valsigna maten
Swedish

今日の食事に感謝いたします.
Kyoo no shoku ji ni kan
sha i ta shi ma su
Japanese

祝　福　食　物
Choo foo sheh oo
Chinese

Abencoe esta comida
Portuguese

Signe maden
Danish

Signe maten
Norwegian

Sivdnit biepmu
Samisk

Zaegen de maaltid
Dutch

Sources and Permissions

Diligent research was done in compiling this book to document the origins of these food blessings. A number of entries are anonymous because there is little knowledge of the authors or works. In many cases relevant sources are no longer available. Every effort has been made to contact original sources. Omissions and errors will be rectified in future editions.

Grateful acknowledgment is made to the authors and publishers for permission to use their copyrighted material.

Prayer 2. Patricia Quintana, with Carol Haralson. *Mexico's Feasts of Life*. Tulsa: Council Oak Books, 1989. Used by permission.

Prayer 3. S. Radhakirshman, ed. and trans. *The Principal Upanishad*. New York: HarperCollins, 1989.

Prayer 10. Courtesy of the Rev. Ann Sutherland Howard, Episcopal Church, United States.

Prayer 11. Arthur Avalon and Ellen Avalon. *Hymns to the Goddess*. Translated from the Sanskrit. London: Luzac and Company, 1913.

Prayer 13. John D. Ireland, trans. *The Itivuttaka: The Buddha's Sayings*. Kandy, Sri Lanka: Buddhist Publications Society, 1991.

Prayer 17. E. V. K. Dobbie. *Caedmon's Hymn and Bede's Death Song* (1937). Reprinted, New York: Columbia University Press, 1942.

Prayer 18. C. Seltman. *Wine in the Ancient World*. London: Routledge and Kegan Paul, 1957. Used by permission.

Prayer 19. The first edition of Saint Cyril's collected works. Ed. J. Aubert, Paris, 1638.

Prayer 20. Text from the *Gelasianum Sacramentarium* courtesy of the Rev. Thomas A. Krosnicki, SVD (Societas Verbi Divini), Divine Word Missionaries.

Prayer 21. Eleanor Shipley Duckett. *Alcuin, Friend of Charlemagne: His Life and His Work*. London: Macmillan, 1951. Used by permission.

Prayer 27. Dante Alighieri. *La Divina Commedia*. Canto XXVI. New York: Alfred E. Knopf, 1993. Used by permission of Christopher E. Knopf.

Prayer 28. Julian of Norwich. *Revelations of Divine Love*. 6th ed. London: Methuen, 1917.

Prayer 30. Poesia Nahuatl archive. 3 vols. National Library of Mexico. Trans. Friar Ángel María Garibay. Mexico City, 1964.

Prayers 31 and 32. John Wallace Suter. *Book of Common Prayer: Our Use of This World's Goods; Prayers for a New World*. New York: Macmillan, 1952.

Prayers 33 and 34. William Joseph Wilkins. *Hindu Mythology: Vedic and Puranic*. Boston: Elibron Classics, 1991. Used by permission of William Joseph Wilkins.

Prayers 37, 38, and 39. Courtesy of the Rev. John M. Allin, twenty-third presiding bishop of the Episcopal Church, United States.

Prayer 55. *The Torah: The Five Books of Moses*. Philadelphia: Jewish Publication Society of America, 1962. Used by Permission.

Prayer 57. Arthur Waley. *Translations from the Chinese*. New York: Alfred A. Knopf, 1941. Used by permission. I am grateful for having access to the private library of Joseph Campbell, whose work in mythology and religion is without peer, and to Richard Buchen, special collections librarian at Pacifica Graduate Institute, who assisted me in discovering this poem.

Prayer 59. Fritz Pawelzik. *I Sing Your Praise All Day Long: Young Africans at Prayer*. New York: Friendship Press, 1967. Copyright © 1967 by Friendship Press, Inc. Used by permission.

Prayer 61. Courtesy of the Embassy of Burkina Faso to the United States.

Prayer 62. Angelus Silesius. *The Cherubinic Wanderer*. Trans. Willard R. Trask. New York: Pantheon Books, 1953. Copyright © 1953 Pantheon Books. Copyright renewed. Used by permission of Pantheon Books, a division of Random House, Inc.

Prayer 69. Benjamin Drake. *Life of Tecumseh, and of His Brother the Prophet: With a Historical Sketch of the Shawnee Indians*. Philadelphia: Quaker City Publishing House, 1856.

Prayer 72. Mildred Tengbom. *Mealtime Prayers*. Minneapolis: Augsburg Publishing House, 1985. Copyright © 1985 by Augsburg Publishing House. Used by permission of Augsburg Fortress.

Prayer 76. Maymie Krythe. *All About American Holidays*. New York: Harper and Bros., 1962.

Prayer 80. Fred Pratt Green. *Hymns and Songs*. Carol Stream, IL: Hope Publishing, 1970. Text copyright © 1970 by Hope Publishing Co., Carol Stream, IL. All rights reserved. Used by permission.

Prayer 81. Abraham Isaac Kook. *Orot Hakodesh: The Lights of Holiness*. Trans. Ben Zion Bokser. Mawah, NJ: Paulist Press, 1978.

Prayer 82. Natalie Curtis, ed. *The Indians' Book*. New York: Dover Publications, 1968.

Prayers 83 and 84. Elémire Zolla. *The Writer and the Shaman: A Morphology of the American Indian*. New York: Harcourt, Brace, Jovanovich, 1973.

Prayer 85. Jerome Rothenberg. *Shaking the Pumpkin: Traditional Poetry of the Indian North Americas*. Garden City, NY: Doubleday, 1972. Reprinted by permission of Sterling Lord Literistic, Inc. Copyright © 1972 by Jerome Rothenberg.

Prayers 87 and 88. Courtesy of the Missionaries of Charity, Calcutta.

Prayer 89. Rigoberta Menchú. *I, Rigoberta Menchú: An Indian Woman in Guatemala*. London: Verso, 1987. Used by permission.

Prayer 90. Charles Langsworth Wallis. *Words of Life*. New York: HarperCollins, 1982.

Prayer 91. Luisah Teish. *Jambalaya*. New York: HarperCollins, 1985. Copyright © 1985 by Luisah Teish. Reprinted by permission of HarperCollins Publishers, Inc.

Prayer 92. Marcia Falk. *Prayer for the Sabbath: Books of Blessings: A Feminist-Jewish Reconstruction of Prayer*. New York: Irvington Press, 1990. Copyright © 1990 by Marcia Falk. Reprinted by permission of Irvington Press.

Prayer 93. O. V. Armstrong and Helen Armstrong, comps. *Prayer Poems: An Anthology for Today*. Nashville: Abingdon Press, 1970. Copyright renewal 1970 by Helen Armstrong Straub. Used by permission of the publisher, Abingdon Press.

Prayer 94. Lyrics by Lawrence Reynolds. Copyright © 1969 by Tree Publishing Co., Inc., and Harlan Howard Songs. International copyright secured. All rights reserved.

Prayer 95. Tony Heilbut. *The Gospel Sound*. Pompton Plains, NY: Limelight Editions, 1997. Used by permission.

Prayer 96. *The Book of Hours*. Overland Park, KS: Congregation of Abraxas, 1985.

Prayer 98. Prayer courtesy of the Rev. John M. Allin, twenty-third presiding bishop of the Episcopal Church, United States.

Prayer 99. Richard Wong. *Prayers from an Island*. Richmond, VA: John Knox Press, 1969. Used by permission.

Prayer 100. Wolf Leslau, trans. *Falasha Anthology*. Introduction by Leslau. New Haven: Yale University Press, 1951. Copyright © 1951. Used by permission of Yale University Press.

Prayers 101 and 103. Courtesy of Bishop Nascisco V. Ticobay, Philippine Episcopal Church, Manila.

Prayer 105. Mildred Tengbom. *Mealtime Prayers*. Minneapolis: Augsburg Publishing House, 1985. Copyright © 1985 by Augsburg Publishing House. Used by permission of Augsburg Fortress.

Prayer 107. Daniel Chanan Matt, trans. Zohar, *The Book of Enlightenment*. Mawah, NJ: Paulist Press, 1983. Copyright © 1983. Used by permission of Paulist Press.

Prayer 108. John Mbiti. *The Prayers of African Religion*. London: Orbis Books, 1976. Used by permission of the Society for Promoting Christian Knowledge.

Prayer 111. George Pullen Jackson. *White Spirituals in the Southern Uplands: The Story of the Fasola Folk, Their Songs, Singings, and "Buckwheat Notes."* New York: Dover Publications, 1965.

Prayer 115. Jack Copley Winslow. *The Eucharist in India: A Plea for a Distinctive Liturgy for the Indian Church, with a Suggested Form.* London: Longmans, Green, 1920. Courtesy of Longman House, England.

Prayer 116. Aylward Shorter. *Prayer in the Religious Traditions of Africa.* New York: Oxford University Press, 1975. Copyright © Aylward Shorter.

Prayer 117. Elizabeth S. Helfman. *Celebrating Nature: Rites and Ceremonies around the World.* New York: Seabury, 1969. Used by permission.

Prayer 118. Courtesy of Sister Judith Marie Saenz, Sisters of the Incarnate Word and Blessed Sacrament, Houston, Texas.

Prayer 119. Starhawk. *The Spiral Dance.* New York: HarperCollins, 1979. Copyright © 1979 by Miriam Simos. Reprinted by permission of HarperCollins Publishers, Inc.

Prayer 120. Iroquois Nation Archives. National Museum of the American Indian Archives, Cultural Resources Center, Suitland, Maryland. Prayer translated by Ely S. Parker in 1851.

Prayer 124. Courtesy of Fr. Joseph L. Asturias, O.P. Dominican Mission Foundation, San Francisco, California.

Prayer 126. James A. Teit. *The Salishan Tribes of the Western Plateaus.* Forty-fifth Annual Report of the Bureau of American Ethnology (1928–29). Washington, DC, 1930. Courtesy of the Smithsonian Institution Press.

Prayer 127. Natalie Curtis, ed. *The Indians' Book.* New York: Dover Publications, 1968. Copyright © 1968 by Dover Publications. Used by permission.

Prayer 128. Copyright © the estate of Chief Dan George. Used by permission.

Prayer 129. Courtesy of Dr. Arthadarshan, the Office of the West Buddhist Order, Norwich, United Kingdom.

Prayer 130. Chinook Psalter. Courtesy of the Chinook Indian Federation, Washington, DC.

Prayer 131. Eido Tai Shinano Roshe, trans. *The Five Reflections*. New York: Zen Studies Society Press, 1982. Copyright © 1982 by the Zen Studies Society Press, New York. Used by permission.

Prayer 132. John Hunter. *Devotional Services for Public Worship*. London: J. M. Dent, 1904. Used by permission of J. M. Dent, Publishers.

Prayer 133. Robert Lowie. *The Crow Indians*. New York: Irvington Press, 1935. Used by permission of Irvington Press.

Prayer 135. Florence Hudson Botsford. *Universal Folk Songster*. New York: G. Schirmer, 1937. Copyright © G. Schirmer. Used by permission.

Prayer 136. Sir James George Frazer. *The New Golden Bough: A New Abridgment of the Classic Work*. Ed. and with notes and foreword by Theodore H. Gaster. New York: New American Library, 1959. Copyright © 1959 by S. G. Phillips, Inc. Used by permission.

Prayer 137. National Geographic Society. *The World of the American Indian*. Washington, DC: National Geographic Society, 1974. Copyright © 1974 The National Geographic Society. Used by permission.

Prayer 138. James A. Teit. *The Salishan Tribes of the Western Plateaus*. Forty-fifth Annual Report of the Bureau of American Ethnology (1928–29). Washington, DC, 1930. Courtesy of the Smithsonian Institution Press.

Prayer 140. Gene Meany Hodge. *Four Winds*. Santa Fe, NM: Sunstone Press, 1979. Courtesy of Sunstone Press, Santa Fe, New Mexico.

Prayer 142. John Lame Deer and Richard Erdoes. *Lame Deer, Seeker of Visions*. New York: Simon and Schuster, 1986.

Prayer 148. Courtesy of Father John Giuliani, the Benedictine Grange, Redding, Connecticut.

Prayer 149. William C. Segal was a personal friend of mine and wrote the prayer for the book at my request.

Index of First Lines

183

Index of First Lines

Index of First Lines

About the Author

ADRIAN BUTASH is a well-known creative and marketing professional and a producer of significant fine arts, television, and film projects. Butash has produced award-winning advertising campaigns and corporate marketing successes for Fortune 500 clients. He is an acknowledged color expert in beauty products and fashion. A graduate of Fordham University, he studied philosophy and cultures of the world. He is also an independent Holocaust scholar who has designed a memorial for the Mauthausen concentration camp. He and his family live in Santa Barbara, California.

Adrian Butash would love to hear from you. He can be reached at abutash2@aol.com.